MEN PSYCHOLOGY. INSIDE AND OUT

5.3188.

Men's being inevitably polygamous is false. If a man loves his woman and she loves him back, sex between the two of them will be such that a third one will not squeeze in between. Men usually cheat out of boredom or resentment, that is, either he does not love or he is not loved.

8.326.

Women like fairytales and wizards. That's why men are divided into tale-tellers and wizards.

6.4869.

In calming a narcissistic jinn down, a woman makes him serve beauty and light, which is something useful and kind. A jinn that has something to do creates. If the jinn is deprived of love, he will start to destroy himself and the world around him.

5.859.

The fruit of a righteous one is the tree of life. A woman joining a sinner will share the sin's infertility with him.

8.305. The way men and women react to conflicts with each other differs greatly.

A woman starts to cry (she feels hurt and scared, and needs to run away), while a man has to handle a conflict by switching off all emotions and fears. A bit later pain goes away, because a woman's task is to live on.

But as for a man, it's the opposite and when the protection gets switched off, he starts to analyze the situation, his pain and suffering may last really long as he can draw reasonable conclusions. The thing is that the strategy of fight implies many variants and it takes time to consider them all, while female strategy of escape is simple and clear, that's why women's pain is always acute (to be remembered) but fleeting.

10.6118.

A beautiful girl has a very positive effect on a boy, motivating him to strive for perfection and strength. Girls love strong, courageous, smart and rich boys. The boy will have to work hard on himself to learn how to earn money and like the girl.

10.5828. Dynamic three-channel encoding

The three-channel programming method works especially well when used by a woman to persuade a man or child to do something.

9.5370. A beauty and a beast.

A man is always a beast but once a woman falls in love with a beast she can turn him into a human being. However, if there is no love in this story, someone will be eaten. It's either a beast who will swallow a beauty or a beauty will torture a beast.

8.332.

Female emotions are the strongest in the first moment and then they fade away ... while it's the opposite with male ones.

5.4049.

Ocytocin is a thing whose absence causes stress and anxiety. By stimulating the production of this hormone in her man and children, a woman makes them feel anxiety and stress, when she has long been absent, and joyful calmness, when she is present.

9.5140.

Men do not like women who are cleverer than they are. That's because men like to be admired, but the intellect does not want to admire the foolishness.

8.580. The essence of muse.

A woman, as a source of desires, is meant to defeat male laziness.

9.4990. It's a big pleasure to give joy.

The more she is happy with him. The more she rejoices at him. The more he manages to make her happy and to bring her joy. Thus the more a man will love this woman.

9.4987.

It's a big pleasure for a man to do something the opposite way. However, all children like to do so.

8.637.

It's only a stupid woman who dreams of becoming a man's meaning of life. The task of any woman is to find a man who already got some meaning of life and become his muse on his way to fulfilling his dream.

9.2326. Technology of hassling.

Repeating the same request constantly, you can make a person do whatever you want.

8.710.

A woman should be easy-going about her man's idiosyncrasies as they hide his source of power.

8.895.

If your man disappoints you, it means you are unable to use him properly.

8.900.

The only handicap that can stop a woman from getting a man is another woman.

9.319.

Figuratively speaking, in order to make a man resemble god, there should be a woman who believes in him.

9.710. Shrek.

Women are monsters who wear masks, while men don't wear masks... Men are beautiful the way they are.

4.1755.

Men's passion for cunnilingus can be regarded as the sign of an extreme form of the desire to possess a woman. Such men are extremely jealous and try, literally, to eat their woman. They are after the woman all the time, limiting her freedom to the maximum, literally devouring her and making her live in the depths of their stomach.

4.3490. Giveaway or a struggle for power.

A woman will fall in love with a man whom she cannot defeat while being sometimes capable of defeating him. Men love in a similar way. This is why truly durable relationships are about both of them constantly quarrelling, making up and winning in turns.

4.3536. Where and how could I meet a man?

On dating sites, write that you have long been dreaming about something, for instance: learn to play court tennis, preference, paintball or Dota 2, go to Tahiti or to the Daisy health camp in suburbs. No matter what. What matters is that you have a dream and you would like to find a man who could fulfil it. For example, you write that you dream of watching all seasons of Star Wars and look for a twin soul. As a matter of fact, there are many ways and places… there are thousands of them – all you need is imagination and courage. A client of ours purposefully found a job at the Federal Rescue Service to be closer to hot, single rescuers.

4.4137.

By letting a man pay for her, a woman provokes in the man the thirst for power and the desire to dominate her. Arrogance is thirst for power, mostly characterized by anger, aggressiveness, jealousy, the suppression of another person's will and so on. What could be more foolish than to become a slave for a handful of coins? – Prostitutes will disagree with you.

4.4158. Boasting.

It's about men's age-old habit of always boasting and sermonizing. On one hand, this annoys everyone and arouses contempt and, on the other hand, women love with their ears. For a woman to love a man, she has to admire how smart and strong he is. One should pay attention to what kind of woman she is. What can amaze her and what can annoy her. It is very dangerous to boast in front of women of high social status. The smarter a woman, the more sophisticated a peacock's beauty should be. The stupider a woman, the quicker she will believe a man's nonsense. All other things being equal, a man has to be very smart and sagacious if he wants to talk to a woman from the top league, i.e. a beautiful, smart and rich woman.

5.2512.

If a female sees no code sequence of words and movements in the ritual dance of a male, she will take him to be the male of a different species and will not let him approach her for mating. A man should inspire and ravish a woman, otherwise this man is not of her species.

5.5080.

As far as excessively persistent men are concerned, there is a theory all girls are familiar with. Such men can only overcome obstacles and immediately lose interest in what is already conquered, that's why having a relationship with these idiots is a very bad idea. And certainly women should not love such men, have children with them or start a family.

5.5133.

A man is delighted to help a woman. An independent woman deprives a man of many joys.

5.5432. Twisting the cow's tail.

A person twisting a cow's tail or untwisting a dog's tail is a person who has nothing to do. Such a person has no intelligence and, consequently, no love and, consequently, no job to do. Such a person is stupid, lazy and steeped in vice. Evidently, a man like this will be focused on lustful thoughts. A lustful bull capable of thinking only about cows.

6.4878. Sink or swim.

Let's make it clear: a husband neurotically in love with his wife will love only her and will not love his child. As a result, the neurotic woman will focus 100% of her love on the child, the husband will get none of her love, and narcotic withdrawals will start driving him crazy. To remedy the situation, the man should consciously give some of his love to the child, and then the woman will give some love back to him.

6.5274.

The reason why men lie and brag a lot is because something small needs female love and affection, and women can only love what they admire. This is why young and immature men always lie; otherwise, without love, they will wither away. However, when they start living together, the man wants the woman to love his real self, warm him up with love and affection and let him grow to the ideal he deems himself to be.

7.1294.

The most important skill for women is the skill of listening men with admiration and excitement. Interest and respect in a woman's eyes inspire a man and make him serve her.

204.

Males usually mean what they say...
without any hidden meaning that
women usually like to grope in their words.

4.87.

The desire of Eros, if you do not find the exit, reborn in hatred of Thanatos.

4.90.

The capacity for ritual is the capacity for love. If a woman sees that a man has dreams and he systematically implements them, then we can hope that he is able to love.

5.77.

A man thinks about sex so often that the question arises when he has time to think about anything else.

5.80. Consequences of female Masturbation.

The property of a man Onanist – "I want everything at once and quickly", but women do not lag far behind men. Is a woman - a Muse she inspires and helps the hero, and sometimes a woman onaniste, it wants to find a ready-made hero. Such a woman does not understand that the hero loves beauty, not women, so a woman can not attract such a man. Therefore, the woman Onanist attracts the men of onanists, men of unprincipled and little capable of exploits, and such a woman does not know how to inspire.

679.

Males are not resistant to flattery. They melt in a puddle from it and flow somewhere.

716.

A man should be a fighter and a creator while a woman should be a helper and a keeper.
And can a woman be a fighter and a creator and a man be a helper and a keeper?
- Yes they can.
- Why?
Because there is both male and female essence present in very person and their proportions hardly depend on sex identity.

855.

The most sacred thing a man can give to a woman is his money...

A man got two passions in his life: a woman and his money. And if he's ready to give her his money, it's a lot like love...

9.34. Virility is the main feature of a hero.

Virile people can overcome fear. This turns them into heroes.

9.46.

A man needs a woman for keeping touch with reality. A man is a potential god-creator, he always tries to create a new world and get lost in it after having lost touch with reality.

9.50. Love and paranoia.

A woman should understand that most men are paranoid and the only thing that can make them sane is female love and gentleness. Otherwise, a man may become a loose cannon who will plunge into anger and grumpiness. That's why it's very dangerous for a woman to get offended by a man and show her irritation or indignation to him… This way a man will see her as an enemy with all consequences it may involve (anger, aggression, attempts to get rid of the aggressor)…

9.55. A manoeuvre.

Experience has shown that there's nothing more stupid than the situation when a man chases a woman. It resembles the situation when a hare chases a lioness and screams "Eat me!"

And generally, it's even silly when a lion chases a lioness. A man is a potential God, his work is to create worlds and not to chase anyone. However, it's not that simple. As we remember that the more we run, the more energy we produce. In other words, a woman is a great reason for working and getting more energy so that to use it for building new worlds later. (The main thing is not to waste it all on women, otherwise this manoeuvre will lose its meaning).

1523. [In brevi]

If a man becomes a victim of female sexuality, charming nature or flirting, natural instincts evoke inside him and the ability to think straight turns off.

1524.

A man's problem is not in alcohol, gambling, women or other human passions. But the problem is in excess and lack of sense of the moderate. Good things come in small packs. And if there are too many good things, the good turns into bad.

Eat an apple to feel fine but eat a hundred of them …and you'll die in pain.

1533.

Male patriarchial attitude, or the desire of a man to care and protect a woman, is probably the strongest male feeling that a woman can use to her advantage.

The desire to care, treat gently, forgive weaknesses, protect and owe - it all is in a man's blood. If a woman manages to show that she belongs to HIM, it's wonderful.

Using «male patriarchial attitude» a woman can skillfully use the following tricks: "blandishment", "give me presents", "a play upon sense of responsibility", "a play upon sense of guilt", "oh excuse me please", "acting like a little girl", "I am blond", "crying", "pretending to feel bad", "help me", "make my work for me", "meet the desires of mine".

Many women (formally) would like to get rid of male ownership over themselves. But the question is why. In a way, this ownership resembles symbiosis. Thus, a man who owns a woman, letting her own herself and making her a part of himself as he starts to care about her, protect her, spend money and feel her as a part of himself...

And a woman, in her turn, by means of purely female tricks rules a man and gets from him anything she wants.

P.s. By the way, patriarchial attitude is in men's blood. And this attitude is given not only to a woman a man considers to be his (but it's much stronger to his woman) but also to other women he knows and treats nicely. Some call it "being a gentleman". In fact, any woman, can skillfully use this male attitude to her advantage.

1534.

Still, in a harmonious relationship a woman can be seen as a man's helpmeet. As a man's experience and role make him a captain while performs the role of a crew. Of course, it can be vice versa but somehow it changes the roles. But still, a woman wants to be cared about and protected as she wants a strong man. As being with a weak man, taking care and protecting him or thinking for him etc., is surely possible but it will hardly bring any family happiness. And of course sex with a man like that will be bad. But sex is one of the free joys in life that shouldn't be underestimated.

That's why it's better for a woman to get the role of a crew and share her man's goals, thoughts, work and plans for the future. In their fight for the place in the sun a couple will become a great team and will live happily together.

Considering this thought deeper, it can be said that it's better for a woman to share the thoughts, ideas and goals of her man, while helping him to achieve goals and inspiring him for feats and deeds to be done... Thus, being like a loyal squire Sancho Panza to Don Quixote to give him a lance when he fights with windmills»... What's more important, is that a man seeing a woman's attention to his ideas and goals and feeling her support, will see this woman as a very precious and loyal person whom he would never like to lose.

1548.

A man really chooses a woman because of sex but in family life he's more interested in comfort, peace, safety, coziness... A man wants his life to become easier and more comfortable. People tend to choose pleasure and avoid negative emotions or problems; but love to be helped, praised, loved and supported. If a woman wants to get married to man some day, she should make him think that his life with her will be easier and more comfortable than without her. That's why women's tricks concerning bitchiness, scandals, jealousy and things like that should be used really carefully during a relationship.

1556.

There's an opinion that men don't like smart women.It should be explained. Actually, everyone loves really smart people, both men and women. And a smart person knows human nature and can make anyone fancy him/herself. A person may be nice, positive and good in every way. People like that are loved and they try to help them and find favor in their eyes. Because people like that know how to get on well with people and live well and talk well.

And it's smart alecs who are not liked. Boastful people and show-offs are not liked as well as those who demonstrate their knowledge proving others to be idiots as compared to smart them. They don't like those who crave conflicts and regularly oppose themselves or suffer from superiority complexes etc.

1561.

Even minimal but regular physical exercises can drastically change a man's looks and health for the better.

It only takes two exercises. Work out abs every day in 2-3 sets and do 8-12 push-ups in 5 sets (or as many as you can). These exercises will make your body beautiful and your posture erect. It trains abs, breast muscles, shoulders, back and arms. With minimal waste of energy and time you get maximal effect for your body and health. The way you look is the way they see you. Where there is a sound body there must be a sound mind. The better you look like, the fewer complexes you have and the more you like yourself and others like you more as well. Women like fit men. And other men will respect you more.

1575.

The best age for a man for getting married is about 30-40 years. That's the age a man gets really mature at. He gets some life experience, gets his fill and maybe first real estate. And the most important thing is that he starts to want to start a family as the thought of his woman being pregnant starts to arouse him. Maybe thoughts like these are the main indicators that it's time to get married and start a family.

What's more, there's some financial wealth necessary for getting married and starting a family. Children are expensive to handle as they demand a lot of attention and take many resources.

One should also take into account the concept of emotional and moral maturity. By this time a man becomes experienced, independent, leaves paternal house and gains some life experience. Generally, it's a big human mistake for a girl to get married to a young man in his 20ies. It can be said that Christ's age is 33 and it's approximately the right age when a man can be trusted.

1581.

What a woman values most about a man is his stability and the power of his libido towards a woman. The power and intensity of his desire to have sex with her. This power influences a man's attraction to a woman and his desire to give her his time and resources. This power influences his ability to forgive her big and small faults. In other words, the task for a woman is to maintain this libido by all means, keeping it from growing weak and fading away. If it fades away, a woman turns from a lover into a sister. Men love sisters too but sisters never get as much love as women they consider desirable.

A man is ready to forgive a lot and give a lot to a woman he wants to have sex with.
However... a woman is also ready to do a lot for the man she loves.

1583.

A woman is attracted to a strong man. A woman is attracted to a real man. A woman dislikes it when a man is insincere, lying, weak, unnatural. A woman dislikes when a man tries to seem someone he's not really is. A man should BE but not SEEM to be.
 That's why if some man has problems with women and women dislike him, then this man should not blame women for it all. This man doesn't even have to read instructive books about how to amuse women. He only needs to BECOME a man. As it's not external sexual characters that make a man a man but rather some inner soul state and women can feel it. As is known, women live by feelings.

1595. Source of pleasure.

Modern life made it possible for a woman to choose a man not only because of money but also because of his soul and other traits.

Nowadays a woman can make money on her own and can protect anyone. So now it's not only money and power that are important about a man. Now a woman may choose, for instance, a soul-mate... or other traits in a man. For instance, kindness, tenderness, care, the ability to be a perfect lover...
It can be said that nowadays a woman needs a man for pleasure...

1609.

The peculiarities of male visual perception: a man sees better into the distance and from above.
The peculiarities of female visual perception: a woman sees better around and next to her.
A man tends to be a visionary far-sighted type while a woman a short-sighted and tactful.
A man performs better under stress when it's necessary to make decisions in a rapidly changing environment.
A woman likes work that implies some exact consequence of particular actions and doesn't like eventualities.

A man has a tendency to experiment, explore new territories and possibilities. A man likes to risk and search. Even his type of thinking implies avoiding stereotypes and cliches.
On the contrary, a woman doesn't like to risk. A woman is more interested in her own territory. A woman prefers to have a one-track mind set for time-tested things. Women like to keep up the traditions and rules and maintain stability.

Two of them together- a man and a woman - form a wonderful symbiosis, a great team.
A man and a woman are like the left and the right hand. They are simply indispensable to each other for successful functioning.

1610.

An interesting thought. During sex a man sees and watches a

woman's behaviour while a woman closes her eyes and feels him...

1625.

A man should always stand by his words, otherwise he's not a man.
A man said it, a man did what he said. If one doesn't want to do it- DON'T say it.

Words should be stood by. You don't want to stand by them? They will make you!
Who will? Life will...

If you said it- be ready to do it. Too late to say no.
And next time you will watch your language.

1626.

A woman's weakness helps a man feel himself strong. In the world where there's no place for feats it can be almost the only reason to be a man.

1636.

In the heart of hearts, boys are scared of girls and feel lack of confidence. It's absolutely normal.

But what exactly are they scared of? Scared of being rejected, laughed at, humiliated. As a rejection for a man is some sort of a tragedy, as if it estimates his male traits as ungraded.

And what should be done to avoid it all. First of all, it's important to be self-confident and not be scared of being laughed at. To do that one should know one's strengths.
It's important for girls what their female friends think about their boyfriends. That's why if a boy wants to be appreciated and not laughed at, he should work things out to be a real man. He should go in for sport, study well and be calm, reliable and just. It's important to dress well and neatly. As well as treat girls with

respect and interest. Thus, girls will be glad to get in touch with a boy like that and his attention will flatter them.

It's also important to remember that a girl is very subjective when estimating a boy. She may be keen on some inner weakness, chemistry, fashion etc. That's why it's always a fifty-fifty chance whether she will like a particular boy or not. Her choice should be taken with poise and rationality. With others equal, if a girl doesn't like a potential candidate to friends, she will be rough and abusive - this way she tries to guard herself from people she doesn't feel like getting in touch with. Such behavior should be taken easy as there are many pretty smart and generally nice girls to choose from and it's useless to be obsessed with those who ignore you.

1637. About the benefits of rudeness.

If a young man tries to get in touch with a girl who dislikes him and if she's generally not in the right mood, it makes her let him know she's not into it. And usually a girl turns rough as she does her best to show a guy she's not interested in him.

Many people say that being rough or aggressive like that is wrong. And that a self-respecting smart girl shouldn't act like that. But the question is why not? As time is money and a man is a creature who can take even any slightest ambiguity as a great chance and may start getting fresh without understanding any hints. That's why if you dislike someone it makes sense to quickly show this person to search for other variants. Such a quick reaction will save a lot of time and efforts.

Again, men are not evil-hearted and if you need a man's help some day, it's always ok to come up and explain you didn't notice his inner advantages at first sight. And this man will have to help...

1642. Male traits typical of a real man:

- Poise and calmness.
- Inner strength and self-confidence.

- Attitude for action and victory. Vigor
- Pep, good spirits.
- Logical thinking. The ability to see real cause and effect chains.
- Good sense of humor.
- Sportiness/fit looks.
- Imagination and broad-minded attitude to things.
- Sense of justice.
- The ability to say «NO».
- The ability to stick to said words.
- The ability to speak sense and clearly. Avoiding unnecessary yakety-yak.
- The ability to get the job done and not leave things undone.
- The ability to care and protect kith and kin.
- Greatheartedness and ability to forgive.
- Generosity.
- Fatalism alongside with planning in coldness of head.
- The ability to see things on a broad scale, not paying attention to rubbish.
- The ability to figure out plan B in any situation. Visionary thinking.
- The ability to think and react quickly to ever changing environment.
- The ability to quickly estimate the real value of things.
- A man should bear stoutly the chances of fortune. And shouldn't weep or drift into pessimism.

Being a hunter, a man should quickly see the goal, estimate its value and quickly try to catch it. It's very important. Otherwise a goal may escape or got caught by other hunters. Next step is to save the goal from being stolen or taken away.
That's why power is very important for a man. As well as sportiness, quick wits, intellect and fatalism.

Many people don't understand what fatalism is meant for. But the hunt is a game. A fifty fifty chance of luck. Bad luck should be taken easy and it's rational to quickly start searching for a new goal to hunt. If losing a game is taken without enough fatalism, it will only make one very upset and lacking confidence and strength. Such a reaction to losing should be excluded.

1644. About male beauty.

Beauty is nice. But it's important to remember "The Beauty and the Beast" fairytale. A beauty of a man is, in the first place, hidden in his soul and actions.

1645.

Signs of intellect can be easily read on the face of a person, in one's eyes or in the way someone speaks... Wisdom is a very beautiful thing.

1649.

As is known, men like fantasy while women like detective stories. It's equal to saying that men like to tell stories while women like to tell tales.

1689.

If a man loses sexual interest in his woman, another woman who will find this interest in him will emerge at once.

1732. Situation. Passive man.

A friend of mine complained about her young man, accusing him of passivity and unwillingness to make decisions and act. Say like says I love you, even jokingly offers to marry, but the steps do not. Still waiting for steps from her. It's like he's some kind of Princess, and he needs to propose. My friend, trying to rouse him, even provoked a love triangle, trying to Wake the young man, make him fight for love and take some steps forward. Instead, he passively surrendered. He said he'd love you forever. Then he went on a binge and got lost. And now the girl doesn't understand what it is all about and how to live with it and fight.

Let's take a close look at this situation. Here, in fact, there are two options:

The man is corny tired of relationships ,... does not want to get married. However, being a weak and indecisive in the face to say it is afraid, so I am glad of any occasion when he would be able to escape, "saving face." He would never say to his face that he was "leaving a girl," he simply did not have the fortitude. He will constantly whine, suffer, write fervent assurances of love and pretend to be a miserable romantic. The truth is, he's just fed up with the relationship, and he's generally glad it happened.

Option the second, slightly more complex. In fact, he wants to continue this relationship, this woman he needs. But ... but ... and another " but." There are many moments in life why he thinks they don't need to be together: he thinks he is too young to marry; he is afraid that his girlfriend is not approved by his relatives and parents; he is afraid that such a marriage will not justify his life hopes and aspirations for career growth and the merger of family capital (perhaps he wants to be related to a more "decent" family, or he simply doubts that this girl is worthy of him); or maybe he considers himself unworthy and fears that he will not cope with such responsibility. In General, the reasons why he does not want to be together, can be many. But that doesn't mean he doesn't love. He may be in love with his soul, but his brain says, " don't." And then a person has a big dilemma: "it seems like you want it, but it also pricks." In such a situation, the person himself can not make a decision. In such a situation, he will suffer, suffer, get depressed, and possibly hinting and whining to her friend that she took decisions for themselves and how to persuade him. He wants his girlfriend to make the decision for him and remove his psychological responsibility for all these "why not".

In such a situation, it all depends on the woman. She had to think about how valuable this man was to her, whether she needed him. Weigh the pros and cons. If need, then simply to accept for him decision and not ask unnecessary questions.

2896.

A man is not an end to a woman but rather a means to the possibility of "feathering a nest and producing nestlings". And it's a man who is supposed to feather the nest and feed the nestlings.

2903.

Beauty is not the most powerful weapon of a woman.
The most powerful weapon of any woman is tenderness.
A man in love doesn't see or hear anything as a man in love can only feel. And tenderness is the best thing to feel.

2969.

The most precious thing that a woman can find in a man is the confidence in the future and the possibility to forget all fears.

2971. Four loved women.

A woman who wants to gain Love, should put up with the fact that she'll never be the only love for her man. A real man always loves four women - his Dream, his Destiny, his Woman and his Job.

3013.

A man looks for beauty, peace and order in a woman. Beauty gives him tenderness and pleasure while peace and order give relaxation.

P.S. Have you ever noticed the beauty and peace of buddhist temples. There are no women there but all men are happy as temples are a substitute for women.

3082.

One should possess spiritual strength to possess power and money.
Spiritual strength is gained in the process of becoming better on the way to perfection. One gains spiritual strength on the way through difficulties to the stars. Going in for sport and study-

ing science also helps one gain spiritual strength. That's why, as a rule, harmonious development of the individual includes both intellective power and physical strength (sport) as well as spiritual power.

P.S.

A man who possesses spiritual strength, also possesses power. Spiritual strength means power. While power attracts money, women and luck.

3187.

Men who have been brought up by their mothers, are careful in an unmanly way.

3192. The killer of dragons.

A real man is someone who kills fears.

3.369.

Persistent in courtship man is good, there is a chance that if you can switch his attention to work, and in business he will also be successful

3.627.

A man, gradually bringing a woman closer, accustoms her to him to the extent that she becomes uncomfortable and anxious without him.

3.686.

Cowardly men have erection problems. They are so afraid of women that the blood goes to their feet and paralyzes the brain. That's why women do not like cowards, sex with them is bullshit.

3708.

Life is like a woman, she does not like smug men. Women love men who love them humbly and selflessly. Every successful man must be moderate, modest, intelligent, noble, just, strong and fearless.

A noble man is beautiful and looks like a flower. Life's goals and objectives like butterflies are attracted to him. The more beautiful Goals a person has chosen, the greater his luck and success, the more he is owed money and health.

Women do not like narcissistic arrogants, do not like those who do not want to serve them. And life, prefers the humble and fell madly in love with the people.

3978.

A loser is a man who hasn't met his muse. The task of a woman is to become the muse for her man and to inspire him into right actions. If a woman fails this task, her man will turn into a loser.

4129. Forbidden fruit and triumph.

It's something forbidden to do that people enjoy doing most.
Tell them what they should not do and they will be set to do it...

The sense of contradiction and desire for freedom.
People are curious and they tend not to trust others' experience and check everything on their own.

And they like to feel themselves winners as well...
As doing things the opposite way is a little (or a big) victory. Victory brings great pleasure and joy. They do things the opposite way just because they're slaves to pleasures.

4.149.

When a woman sees an immature and weak man, she instinctively feels attracted to him, because at the level of the subconscious feels that if you warm the chicken with your love, it can grow into a great cock.

4.153.

An immature man is weak and cowardly, but if he finds a woman who loves him and saves him from fear by getting rid of fear, such a man can grow up and know the world.

4.155. Start with yourself.

For a woman to bring an immature man to maturity, she herself must be Mature. The task of a woman is to raise not only a child, but also a husband.

4.162.

A woman should avoid men who believe that their parents owe them something. A man takes his eternal, that "all he needs" a woman and becomes unbearable, aggressive and touchy. A person who believes that someone owes him something is by nature a degenerate, unsuitable for a relationship.

4.163.

Mama's boy, men of this type are so vile by nature that they cause nothing but contempt and a desire to spit in his face. A woman should not be restrained by such men. You should show him contempt and other negative emotions. Only the awareness of their own inferiority will give a chance to this subhuman grow up.

4223. A note for a muse.

Love inspires to heroism and brings good luck.
A man who is loved, is capable of many things.

4224.

A woman is able to inspire a man in two ways:
it's either a man who can choose her as his muse
or a woman herself can choose a man for love and support...

4.229.

The woman, wanting to rule over men, forever leaves his immature childlike state. To Mature, a man must avoid them for a long time, otherwise he will remain a child forever. A man's dependence on a woman turns him into a child.

4.448.

A man only seems, that he wants sex, money and power. In fact, he wants children, and for that he wants the love and admiration of women who would love him and give birth to his children. However, the woman wishes same.

4.570. Smart and strong woman.

The mind implies humility, and the lack of humility turns the mind into stupidity. A clever woman knows all about men, their boasting, their vanity, and their vices. A clever woman knows that she needs to be admired for love, but she cannot admire a deeply vicious husband... What could she do? Alone sad and cold, lacking love and affection. A clever woman uses the tool "humility", she will accept the imperfection of a man, rightly believing that a green banana will ripen in the store.

4.597.

Men intuitively like to underestimate the self-esteem of their women, because self-belief is the power of movement, and intimidated and insecure woman stiffens with fear and does not try to escape. From fear she loves. She fades from fear, ceases to attract other men.

4.703.

If a woman wants an obsessive man to stop loving her, she should put him a crazy price for sex and then he screamed " prostitute!"leave her alone. Tell him you don't love him, but you love his money, and he'll stop loving you.

4.802. Mama's boy.

A rather mischievous type of man that any sensible woman should avoid. How do you know such a man? He has many traits.

He hates or loves his parents too much. He believes that someone that he's got and loves to throw mud at others. Always whining and dissatisfied. Demands pity and begs for love and attention. Often such a man is not independent or lives with his parents, is tedious and prone to reflection. Often it is one child in the family, younger or later child.

At first, such a man may seem attractive, because a woman feels his fear of women and his weakness, and therefore is not afraid of him. Plus, these beleaguered mothers children can grow in good careerists, achieve some success, get a good education and academic degrees. However, it should be understood that all this is from the evil one. No degree or big salary will make a decent person out of a degenerate. Theoretically, with a deep knowledge of psychology and a lot of love, you can make a person out of it, but it will be difficult. Other things being equal, we guarantee you a life in hell.

5.105.

The Princess and the sex of the Kingdom in addition is a symbol of love. A man who has found his love will find his Kingdom.

5.416.

When a man makes a breakthrough, he is waiting for a collision with someone who will slow him down. Hardness of the man, meeting after breakthrough softness of the woman, gets bogged down in a bog.

5.422.

Success in many areas of human life of men with homosexual orientation is due to the fact that they managed to avoid the trap of female softness, restraining male hardness. In the absence of female resistance, male hardness was able to grow into the sky, and serve beauty without unnecessary interference. A homosexual is essentially a celibate monk whose strength lies in avoiding the swamp of feminine softness.

5.599.

According to statistics, most men would not mind becoming a woman, but women who want to become men are much less. So to live well?

5.612.

The soul is a woman's essence, the mind is a man's. A man who lives by the impulses of the soul is like a henpecked man.

7.177. Non-inspiring woman.

Many women believe in male greed, they say, they do not want to spend money on them, on the house, on children. The point is that a man associates children and home with a woman, and if the woman herself does not inspire, then any expenses associated with her do not cause any joy or desire.

7.384.

Sexual abstinence increases male aggressiveness. Aggressiveness is related to motivation, which is generally useful. However, if the family with sex problems, the husband will be very aggressive to his wife, which will cause many problems.

7.387.

The main reason for the aggressiveness of men is hunger. If a man lacks food or sex, he becomes extremely angry and churchgoers on all growls.

7.390. Taming a wild beast.

Sex and tenderness are the tools with which a woman can maintain a man's loyalty to her. A man who lacks affection and sex becomes angry, aggressive and does not want to serve.

7.397.

It is known that a man's brain grows to 25 years, respectively, the average age of a Mature human soul about 25 years. They say women's souls are a little younger, but it needs to be checked.

7.457.

A man is a wild freedom-loving beast, to domesticate him and tame him, forcing him to serve himself and his family, a woman requires a special art. Women's tools for the domestication of men is the love, tenderness, admiration, beauty, sex, moral support, etc. If a woman neglects these tools, the man again wildly and run away from the family.

7.570.

An independent woman is a woman who does not need a man around. Men don't like women who don't need them.

7.571.

A woman to keep a man, you need to either need him or be useful to him, helping him, and it is better that all this was at the same time. A relationship in which no one is needed and useless is dead.

7.862.

The problem with an intelligent woman is that she sees her man's flaws very well, which prevents her from admiring him and, consequently, from loving him.

7.879.

A man needs a dream and a woman who will share this dream with him in order to achieve success in life.

7.881. Tractor and rocket fuel of love.

A woman needs to find a man with a dream to share with him. Helping and encouraging a man to follow his dream, a woman will be able to realize their dreams.

8.274.

The advice saying that the right guy is not worth fighting for was given by women who got no men of their own and they regularly have to use other women's men.

8.309.

Female emotionality: she should run away. Male calmness and rage: he should attack.

8.356. A working recipe.

In order to calm down your man- keep silent, smile a little and caress him...

8.368.

A man's reaction to problems and threats should be without unnecessary emotions - calmly, perhaps with anger and rage but definitely without submission or signs of weakness.

8.383. Hunter instinct.

Some feel like chasing something that runs away.

8.598.

A magician differs from a tale-teller by the ability to do miracles instead of just telling about them.

8.717.

Obsession, insanity and bigotry are the words that lead a man to success at what he does.

8.843.

The tip about wearing beautiful underwear to warm the heart is effective for men as well.

8.878.

In a relationship between a man and a woman the marriage-bed is not as important as personal faithfulness. As it doesn't matter who sleeps with whom but what matters is trust, mutual care and devotion.

8.885.

A man can barely resist a woman who holds control over her sexiness.

8.907.

Generally, I agree that the initiative for a relationship should come from a man as it's only up to him to decide whether he likes a particular woman or not. Otherwise, he may agree to flirt only because of the general interest to women.

9.114.

It's much more difficult to stop a man from reproduction rather than a woman. Thousands of spermatozoa are like a missile blow but there's only one ovum.

9.523.

You don't need to chase women. Firstly, it's a sexual imposition and secondly, better let them chase you.

9.528.

In order to help a man become a Creator, there should be a woman who believes in him.

9.533.

Usually, a man is a Creator and a woman is his Angel.
Usually, a man is a Destroyer and a woman is his Demon.

9.616.

A dream is the only thing that a man should really chase... Of course, it's also possible to chase women, pleasures and food, but I wouldn't recommend to waste energy on silly things.

9.653.

Don't get me wrong, bird doesn't sing beautifully without reason, it wants sex.

9.681. Idealism is meant for pretty girls, others need pragmatism.

Idealism is meant mostly for girls. Beautiful girls are loved automatically, while boys need to get and conserve energy.

3.1310.

Jealousy is a woman's great weapon to control weak and insecure men, turning them into her slaves.

3.1440.

The strong are not afraid to be weak, but the weak always push and inflate.

3.1956. Eternally dissatisfied woman, and idealistic.

Men are idealists doomed to a scandalous conflict society and women. For nothing will keep such a man near a woman, except the knowledge of his inferiority and remorse.

3.1967. A grain of sand.

The metaphor of a Genie living in a bottle, is a metaphor for men and women Gina shell, which, freeing the Genie out of the bottle, offers him to become a pearl in the shell.

3.1986.

Man and woman idealists is the two fire, which is cold, and to warm up, they bask each other. The main thing in this matter is to keep a distance.

3.2063.

A man likes to be considered good, and the more he is considered good, the more he wants to appear good.

3.2064.

A person remembers that he was bad and now his conscience torments him and he wants to do something good to get rid of guilt.

3.2065. Chameleon and butterfly.

A woman is a chameleon and a man is a balloon. The woman with all the different and her a lot, but man it's a butterfly that knows that she's a worm.

4.1143.

Women are more realistic than men. Reason? They're perfect. Men are more aware of their inferiority, more fantasize and soar in the clouds. Dreams make men grow.

4.1287.

Immature people want love in the form of admiration for themselves, if they and their actions are not admired, they are extremely offended. In fact, such men are looking for and maternal admiration-unconditional love from any woman.

4.1304.

Loving is like driving a car: seeing everything, feeling everything. A man who loves his car, notices every detail, scratch, dirt... and corrects, and brightens. Women love men in beautiful cars, because if a man treats his car well, there is a chance that he knows how to love a woman.

4.1442.

They say baldness is a sign of debauchery and voluptuousness. Libertines suffer from baldness more often than other men. I wonder why?

4.1522.

Passionate and loving man is not suitable for a serious relationship, because, accustomed and sated with love, he will fall out of love and run away to look for another woman. You need a man who's in love with his dream. If you share his dream with him, he, like a mother who loves her child, will love the woman who will share his love with him.

4.2005.

A woman should not be afraid to be a durra. Men are not afraid of fools and love to teach them and help them, and this, as you remember, a great opportunity to meet. Men are happy when there is someone to teach, they really like women who take their teachings with their eyes wide open. Make your man happy, let him teach you.

4.2303.

A narcissistic husband chooses a weak and dependent woman who is ready to admire him, but will constantly urge and pull him that he is doing something bad and wrong. Bad love, bad perform the duties of a father and husband, little work. Husband to yell and snap. In General, everyone will get what he deserves.

4.3521.

The main problem of a smart woman is that it is difficult for her to find a man worthy of reproduction. A smart man doesn't want to admire anyone.

4.3714. Toxic man. Which men should be avoided.

Neurotic, deceitful and weak men should be avoided. Immature and unsuitable for relationships men do not know how to love, do not know what love is. These are narcissistic men, they consider themselves the most intelligent, do not read books, and if they read, then only artistic or narrow-profile. They are very vain and proud, always whining and complaining, scolding everyone, not happy with everything, surrounded by mostly fools and scoundrels or, conversely, some Holy people. Because these people read little and are inherently ignorant, they cannot communicate, they cannot talk, they cannot behave in society... they cannot do anything. It's just teenage children in adult bodies. The body may be 30-40 years, and the soul 12. Such "CHILDREN" are looking for new "MOMS" to love them, take care of him and have sex. They can be found on stickiness, moaning and whining vespasiano with love and sex.

We also recommend avoiding schizophrenics, chronic neurotics, immature people, sissy boys, daffodils, people with inferiority complex and megalomania. Of course, we understand that it is difficult to find a normal man, but they are, we have seen them many times and recommend you not to give up.

4.3878. How to choose a man for a relationship.

This man should have a dream and a favorite thing. He likes to read books in the genres of non-fiction, Economics, psychology and philosophy. He has a favorite business, he is busy with something. If the only desire of this man is to find a woman who will love him, then you need to run away from him as far as possible. The only exception is if you are ready and able to raise children. Love and tenderness can make an immature man Mature. However, the high art of love requires special skill and wisdom. Other things being equal, avoid men who love or hate their mommy too much.

4.4149. Why does a man like me, then closer, then moves away.

It's a classic neurotic relationship. When two neurotics encounter their passion head-on, after a while they become addictive and need to step back to restore the sensitivity of dopamine receptors. This can be fought, but the tactics of the fight requires strategy and careful study of the details.

4.4150. Likes or dislikes.

Immature man loves only himself and his pleasure. Deprive him of pleasure, and he will become furious, begin to be rude, swear, whine. Real Mature men, suitable for such a cheap provocation will react with dignity. Again, real love is not hiding, not afraid, not greedy, no doubt, and If a man says he loves me, but do not want to marry, – please send him to hell. If he really does, he'll come crawling up on his knees with a ring in his hand.

4.4153. A man does not trust me and is jealous, what to do?

Abandon him and find another. He's an immature man, too young to be in a relationship. He loves no one but himself and his pleasure. Of course, you can leave him and suffer with him all his life or take him under the arm of a psychologist, so he worked out with him. But he will not go to a psychologist, he will not correct himself, and you will spoil your whole life by ditching it on a puppy with an inferiority complex. Such easy to know they are suspicious, distrustful, aggressive, vile, all criticize and criticize, etc. on the other hand, you can warm it with love and tenderness. People believe those they love. However, you need to make sure that your love is deserved, otherwise he will begin to doubt himself and you.

4.4156. If you're being chased by a man, what do you do?

Immature and neurotic men can not survive when they are abandoned, and turn into obsessive manic jerks. Like hysterical children, they cry, whine, snot, threaten suicide, swear, get angry, lick your feet or, conversely, pour mud. In General, behave extremely on-beastly. What to do? We need to understand that these are very weak men, and all their threats is the crying of a child who was deprived of candy. No need to feel sorry for them or listen. It's all a lie, even if you foolishly go along with him and take him back, as soon as he achieves his goal, he will fall out of love with you. That's the way they are, kids, they cry when they don't have candy, but when they give it to them, they throw it away. Therefore, there are no options... This man must be removed from life.

Where to start. First, delete and block all of his contacts in your phone and social networks. Secondly, do not make contact, do not talk, do not regret. Forbid anyone to approach you. Not agreeing to a meeting, not getting in the same car, not being alone. At the meeting completely ignored. When trying to call You - hang up. If a person does not understand the words, warn him that a statement will be written to the police, reported to him at work and in the neuropsychiatric clinic.

Especially well, when this man starts to threaten You or whine that hang himself, strangle and throw himself out the window. It is good to record such recognition on a voice recorder or take a screenshot of the emails. Print it all out, and when you write an application for it, attach it all. The point is that the threat of suicide is psychiatry and, therefore, forced hospitalization and psychiatric registration. This is a yellow ticket and the inability to find employment in the civil service, work with people, etc.

If a person even after that does not calm down, he will be forced hospitalization. Warn the man that if he does not stop chasing you, he will face an extremely sad fate. And if he doesn't understand, go to the police and the neuropsychiatric clinic with a statement about the threat of suicide and socially dangerous behavior. Pre-find out the exact name, address and place of work of this person to all the data immediately went to his place of residence and work.

5.1354.

Every man in his life hundreds of times thought and about pedophilia, and about how, to become woman, and about homosexuality, and about cloud other sins and vices. Of course, men are afraid of their thoughts and only fear restrains them. Fear causes aggression and denial.

5.1689. Scene from Ramayana.

A man is a hunter who crosses borders for the sake of rich booty which he wishes to present as a gift to his beloved.

5.2066.

Stress is fear. Cowardly men, unable to control their fears and anxieties, are 3 times more prone to cardiovascular disease than women.

5.2534. The nature of male infidelity.

A man cheats on a woman because he can't be biologically sure she's not cheating on him. When you have 1-2 children from one woman, the biological risk is too great that they will die or they are from another man, so natural instincts force a man to be safe at all costs.

5.2980.

Running after women, a man recovers excess energy and time, which he apparently has nowhere to go.

5.2989. Chronicle of the loser.

A man always serves its dream and if his dream-woman, then all his money and time this woman and inherited, and when love end, will remain this a man nor with than...

5.3689.

The female manner to adapt to all tastes and ideas of the man steel chains chains the man to it. Men are vain, finding a soul mate, they can not live without it.

5.4557.

A woman falls in love when she gives up, when she can't stand the onslaught. A man, on the contrary, loves until he surrenders.

5.5074.

Women do not like obsessive men, because obsession is a sign of immaturity and inability to love. Other signs of immaturity are suspicion and aggression. That's what stupid kids and teenagers do, but not Mature men.

5.5137.

Love woman to man is a woman's admiration of her man and the desire to immortalize it by creating a offspring. A woman wants to multiply what she likes.

5.5335.

A beautiful woman creates a romantic mood in a man. In a romantic mood, a man is willing to spend more money than usual. A man really wants to make a nice beauty, to brag to her, to demonstrate his power and steepness.

5.5338.

Men are more likely to choose less here and now, and women then more. Women who know that children grow for a long time, willing to suffer long for the sake of beautiful hope.

6.2116.

Someone told the woman that by denying her husband sex, she would preserve his passion for years. Maybe so, but whether she will keep her husband for years is a very big question.

6.3140.

Cowardice turns men into women. Effeminacy is a consequence of a lack of testosterone. A fear hormone, cortisol, inhibits sensitivity to testosterone that leads to fullness and deprive men of virility.

6.4574.

For a man, sex is a symbol of power, it supports the integrity of the illusion of his "I", the feeling that the woman belongs to him, a part of him.

6.4988.

It is desirable for a woman to look for a relationship such a man who loves his job and has a dream, then there is a chance that such a man can love several things at once.

6.4991.

If a man with a dream fell in love with a woman, there is a chance that he knows how to love several things at once. Such a man is able to love his wife and work at the same time, or his wife and child at the same time. If a man is so passionate that he loves only a woman, it is likely that either all his other Affairs will go to waste, or he will grow cold to his wife to be able to serve his other purposes.

6.5276. Books little read, there is no truth in psyche.

Men who are forced to lie to women about themselves and promise them everything they want, want at all costs to attract the attention of women to themselves. Male ghouls can not live without women's love and attention, it is their only source of energy, because inside themselves there is an absolute emptiness.

6.5873. Love without awareness is sin.

A woman should love a man's mind. If a man's spirit is not admirable and firm, it is a sin to love such a man, and the woman who loves him is doomed to suffering. A man weak in spirit and full of doubt and fear is a lie, and one who loves him is doomed to suffer and pay for his sins.

6.6024.

If a man is strong and rich, a woman will want sex from him and there will be many children. Such a woman will be annoyed that a man gives her very little time. The problem is, that force and wealth men in Affairs his and on woman time will a bit.

6.6025.

Man daily activities absolutely necessary for three reasons. First, it is a good reason to take a shower every day. Second, it relieves stress, the source of all human suffering and disease. Thirdly, it is the subduing of the passions of the body and the key to the beauty of the body. A man with a beautiful strong body is always sexually attractive to women.

6.6368.

If a man is not able to offer a woman anything but pleasure and entertainment, he will not be able to be interesting to her for a long time. Vice is decay, and women love anything that grows and only when it grows. A woman needs a growth factor, otherwise she will become bored, and she will lose sexual interest.

6.6370.

There are two types of men, the first grow and therefore honest, strong and joyful, and the second does not grow, from which they always lie and suffer.

6.6502.

Muse the one that can infect man and dreams to get a man to love yourself to fulfill them.

7.1018. A defective man.

A woman needs a man who has a high purpose in life. People who have no high purpose in life are quarrelsome, unreliable and prone to vices.

7.1353. Female hypnosis.

Woman desirable focus attention his men on itself, for, if she will lose this attention, fish can feel freedom and run.

7.1357. Sweet as honey, woman.

A woman needs to be gentle, beautiful and diverse in order to keep the attention of her man. Men are curious, their attention is constantly looking for new and they, like fish, swim where they look. Having lost the attention of a man, a woman quickly loses the man himself.

7.1358.

Sweet as honey, a woman attracts the attention of a bee, a man can not tear himself away from her, except when the honey runs out.

7.1365.

Empathy allows a woman to feel what a man wants from her and, by giving it to him, turn a happy victim into a drug addict and his faithful servant.

7.1496.

Some weak women like shy men, because it seems to them that if he is shy, then weak, then not terrible, then he can not be afraid and even can be controlled.

7.1522. A man surrounded by good and intelligent people.

Knight without fear and reproach is a strong man who conquered fear, next to which is not scary, plus he does not blame anyone for anything and does not reproach about and without.

7.1645.

It is good when the girl eats little, otherwise a man can be tortured by the fear that she will eat all his money.

7.2216.

I heard a story about a smart woman, who used to refuse her husband intimacy when he was complaining about his diseases. They say, this good man was known for his excellent health.

7.2542.

A woman does not have to marry a man she is not ready to admire, not ready to love, and therefore not ready to serve him. Accordingly, a man should not marry a woman who does not love him.

7.2630.

A man's need to conquer a woman speaks of his helplessness. In the first place, he is the slave of his pleasure, and in the second place, he seeks in woman the source of his power.

7.2853.

A man who can't protect a woman from her fears doesn't need her.

7.2859. Repentance of a sinner.

For a man to go mad with jealousy, his fear of losing a woman must become real, he must believe in it. He must believe that a woman has put a cross on him and on her knees begging for forgiveness. However, for this scenario to work-you need to clearly know that he is infected with love. If a fish loves a worm, it will not fall off the hook.

7.2861.

To return a man-you need to turn off the passion and achieve passionlessness. For the passionate are full of fear of losing their passion. And fear makes them slaves to their passion. Slaveholders rarely love their slaves. Moreover, a man who feels himself a full-fledged master of a woman loses the fear that she will run away and can afford too much. Again, feeling his power, he does not feel the need to spend energy caring for her. He must feel threatened by the loss of power.

The woman to get out of the vicious circle of their relationship, you should get rid of the fear that it engenders - the passion. It is necessary to achieve peace of mind. When a man feels that there is no fear in a woman, he will become infected with the fear of losing her.

7.2862. How to drive a man crazy with jealousy.

The mechanics of the case with the departed girlfriend was the following - she left, and he suffered withdrawal. She probably had a fight with him before the trip, told him that he was a rag and, after leaving, ignored him, and he fell "into withdrawal." And week this was bad. Then she came and he was released, he tried to curry favor with her and he felt better. But the withdrawal from you began to grow. My suggestion is not to break him, but to ignore him and keep aloof. To put pressure on his remorse and guilt that he made children here, now there ran to do that than such a life-it is easier to die, and everything will be to blame for him, because he is not a man.

But you can not let him go and allow to leave. As it is emotionally to show the alienation, to cause jealousy some, but not to let go and the words to associate his behavior with her, they are what they eat, what they are the twists, how he wants, but he is not a man - abandoned children, etc. That is, as if to associate their behavior with the competitor. And that when you die of hunger-he will be free at all and can make a new children. So you can't let him accuse You of treason. Such accusations should be said that he is a traitor. And if he hopes for something, you need to go to a family psychologist together, perhaps this will allow You to accept the situation.

7.2863. The suspension hurts, the man attacks the pain.

7.2864.

In most cases, the natural intuitive behavior of a woman with her man is correct and depends on the characteristics of this man. The problem happens if you overreact. Need some balance angel and demon, carrot and stick, justice and injustice, rational and irrational, love and dislike, closeness and distance. Balance is when both opposing entities exist simultaneously.

7.2867.

When a man says woman "hate" - this means, that he likes its, and its coldness causes him pain. And if women flee from pain and hatred, then men, contrary, attack adversary, the more, running away. After all, the woman, sensing his hatred, either freezes in horror or runs away. A man, seeing such a situation, feels an irresistible desire to catch up with her. A woman should escalate the situation to the limit and at some climax demand that he surrender and accept all conditions in return for her return.

7.2870.

The essence of the relationship between a man and a woman is that the man himself can hardly control his desires, and he needs an external system of checks and balances. The purpose of women-to manage the desires of men, directing them in the direction of improvement, development, work, home and family. A woman should help a man control his passions. They say the woman is the Keeper of the fire. Fire is passion. Focusing on a part of the man's passion and driving it, the woman rules over fire.

7.2876.

A woman cannot control a man, but she can control a man's passion.

7.2877. Absolute love is absolutely corrupting.

The primary weakness of women is pride. Controlling passion, a woman acquires absolute power over a man and falls into pride.

The man, feeling the loss of freedom, falls into a rage. In this case, a woman can save modesty, having absolute power over a man, she should inspire him with the illusion of freedom and even a sense of some power over a woman.

7.3177.

A decent man is busy with his own Affairs, so he has no time to run after women. Therefore, if a woman needs a decent man-she herself will have to find and catch him.

7.3269.

As you know, Solomon's wife eventually became the Pharaoh's daughter Bithia. Their wedding coincided with the completion of the Jerusalem Temple, the main cause of Solomon's life. Metaphorically, it was Solomon's reward. It is said that to seduce him, Bifia danced 80 different dances in front of him and thousands of musicians played sweet music. How could Solomon not to succumb to the seduction? History, in fact, is standard: once a man reaches greatness, having finished the main thing of his life, the best women begin to show him very active attention, which not everyone can resist. The passion into which Beefy had turned was like a conflagration sweeping away everything in its path.

7.3682.

7.3707. Only a strong husband can take the child, the weak can not.

Men often threaten ex-wives to take their children, but do it very rarely, because they are weak. Only a very strong man can take a child. Weak men are afraid of children and they are very expensive for them.

7.4055.

Deny sex to your man a woman should be wisely, so as not to offend him. Keeping the balance of desires and opportunities, you should not just refuse, but promise more tomorrow than less today.

7.4278.

Male tyrants humiliate their women in order, given their low self-esteem, to further lower it and force it to serve themselves. But that's very rude. There are plenty of more elegant ways to lower people's self-esteem than just insult them. It is possible, for example, to rise so high that the person next to you will be so small that he will automatically want to serve you. When you underestimate a person's self-esteem, he wants to achieve peace, he wants you to feel sorry for him. He'll do a lot for your praise.

7.4411.

A midlife crisis is when a man in his thirties begins to realize that he has been cruelly deceived. He works a lot and well, and the happiness both was not, and no.

7.4412. Dumb.

The main slave of modern society is the father, and this is a silent slave, who even took away the right to complain.

7.4499.

A man accustomed to obey orders and the woman, of course, it would be necessary to use it. The man waits for demands and instructions, but the woman is interested in his desires. She wants him to want what she wants and guess what she wants. The source of women's desires-stereotypes and templates, books and movies, friends, sisters, mom and parent family. The man in this situation saves that in principle if to think, desires at the woman not so much. Of course, if desire to perform small, grow large.

7.4506.

What is a drunk man? Male drug addict? Is a man a slave to his small and great pleasures? This is an emotionally castrated man, a man deprived of his dignity and lost faith in himself. Who castrated him? Many who could, but mostly this wife, parents, state, somewhere at work or pieces of broken dreams.

7.4507.

Let's be fair: if a man is emotionally castrated and deprived of his dignity, he is the one to blame because he gave up and fell into dejection. Considering, however, that what has been castrated is a metaphysical phallus, a new, fresh, juicy and green phallus will grow anew if that man picks himself up and wracks his brains.

7.4508.

Hysterical women are very fond of obsessive men, but do not know how to use them. Although, of course, they are suitable for each other. For example, a narcissistic man does not fit a hysterical woman categorically.

7.4551. The man of her dreams.

If the girl did not have a father, her expectations about men will be perfect and not softened by reality. Such a girl will expect from men what she was expecting from his mother, plus some ideal and illusory images created by her mother, books, friends, movies, etc. the Man of her dreams is a kind of an idealized collective image of men mom and dad in one person. Such a girl will be very difficult to take the image of a real man, very far from ideal.

7.4555.

A man perceives the house as a place of women's requirements, and the more such requirements, the less you want to go there.

7.4797. Avoid people who have no dreams and goals in life.

A man who has no business is inherently vicious. A man needs his work. Women have more choices... She can find a man with her business and help him, start her own business or concentrate on family and children.

7.5110. Fear breeds a lack of sense of proportion.

A woman, trying to bind a child or a man to her, turns them into monsters. The reason is the lack of a sense of proportion and fear. Trying to deliver joy, the woman herself receives this joy, which causes dependence on all participants in this process. This dependence ties people together as a community. However, if a woman is neurotic and full of fears, she will use this weapon beyond measure, which will lead to the development of processes whose symptoms coincide with severe cases of drug addiction. There is a degradation of personality, aggression, resentment, mutual hatred, paranoia and fear.

7.5465.

Choosing a man, a woman should carefully look at his dreams and goals, work and even entertainment. Either she would share his passions with him and support them, or they would destroy her.

7.5489.

Never, under any circumstances, should a woman choose to marry a man who is socially or culturally inferior to her. In the Vedic tradition, this behavior led to the conversion of untouchables and the woman and her children. From the point of view of psychology, this state of Affairs is justified, those who faced, will agree with it.

7.5496.

A woman should talk to a man by hints. A man, after decoding a hint, treats it like his own thought. A man resists direct thoughts treating them as order, aggression and violence. However, if a man is weak, neurotic or silly, so he can't get any hints, one should talk to him straight off. And If a person doesn't even understand words you say you should talk to him by force.

7.6048. Spiritually Mature man.

In Buddhist countries, no decent girl will marry a man if he has not been a monk in a monastery for at least a year or two.

7.6387.

A man who agrees to live with his wife's relatives is called a fool. However, the one who lives with her, too far gone from the first.

7.6590.

Deceived, so cheated, so men lie.

7.7415.

Ugly is all that is different from the standard. A standard is something that is perfected first. For example, a boy fell in love with his first female image seen in a photo or TV. This image formed a great reference, but a Platonic way. Then all the other women will be compared to him. And the removal from it will cause pain, but attract attention. Attention is love, so this person will fall in love with the opposite, and reach for the reference.

7.7525. Immaturity.

Noticed that infantile women really swear by infantile men, saying that they can't make the first (second to tenth) step and seduce them. Infantile people are very upset by the fact that no one wants to lead them and make them do what they really want.

8.1017.

For a man, His war is the most important thing.

8.1036. Priority of values

The idea that a woman and a family can come first for a man is silly. His Cause always comes first for a man. Serving his woman? What nonsense...For a man, his woman is his property, source of joy and helper. His right hand, who is responsible for home, children and many other important things. He values his woman, loves her, cares for her – like a good owner cares for his property. Your own is useful and pleasant to your eye. Woman is a helper, friend, lover, muse, source of energy, joy and inspiration. But for a woman, her husband, house, children and family should come first. Why so? Because it's her Cause. And Cause always comes first for a person.

On the other hand, if a woman has other Causes, while a man doesn't have any, Family may become such a man's cause. If spouses agree, so be it.

8.1037.

To start a family, a woman needs to find a man who has a dream and share it with him, and then quietly load him with her own dream. If he can handle one dream, he will be able to handle two ones as well.

8.1038. Purely female dreams.

As for a man, the goal or the dream to find love and start a family seems to be very silly.

8.1040.

Of course, men of nowadays got worse and became somewhat weak as they can't even handle their women.

8.1056.

Taking into account the concepts of Yin and Yang, men and women, black and white, good and evil... Can we suppose that angels and demons are like men and women or vice versa?

8.1117.

It's only love that can win the triumph over evil. Human evil nature is the direct consequence of need for love. They really lack love and it makes them evil.

8.1151. Priceless prince.

I noticed that female dreams and desires concerning men and life are very alike. A perfect man is the one who wouldn't control or limit a woman's freedom, wouldn't try to change her but would take her as she is. And would listen to her opinion. He should be fun to talk and go out with to. He should be tactful at getting fresh...
If only he was kind, tall, rich, smart, caring... then he would be above any price.

8.1283.

A man needs a woman who would have confidence in his abilities while women love men who they can have confidence in.

8.1309. A useless man.

A man in someone else's house is not a master...

8.1428.

The power of samurai is in the beauty of his soul and his soul resembles a garden near his house.

8.1460.

A woman is a god to a man, a man is a god to a woman. Angels of the man god are women. Angels of the woman god are men.

8.1736.

A man is quite an aggressive self-affected animal, however he can be useful for a woman as a source of all sorts of usefulness and pleasures. It's useful to get a man, but it's necessary to learn how to master his rage and use him which includes a thorough research into the operation manual.

8.1743.

The main opponents of male chauvinism are fathers who have daughters. Thus, the war between the sexes is unequal.

8.1753.

A man who treats his woman badly, commits a heavy sin that will make his things get in a degraded condition. Spending time and money on women makes karma better and brings good luck that will bring even more money than it was spent.

8.1762.

The fact that a man got a beautiful woman, speaks for his great power.

8.1906. A woman is a source of a warrior's power.

8.1967.

The main crowning glory of a man is his Business.

8.2108. Be careful what you wish for.

The decrease of male aggressiveness in society leads to a decrease in quality of sex and female sadness.

8.2292.

Men wear masks to hide their monster, while a woman is the mask that she wears. Besides, there are quite many masks of hers.

8.2312.

Will and intellectual power glorify a man, while beauty is glorious for a woman. Thus, women are form, men are content.

8.2416.

A man should rather make things than children.

8.2688.

Women's expenses greatly inspire men's income.

8.2709.

They say that a real man is the one you can feel calm with. But doesn't calmness mean death?

8.2727.

An unskillful woman tried to tame and rule a wild man but she did it badly, as a result he got mad and nearly swallowed her. Who is to blame?

8.2836.

If you're a man, you should figure out your own feat to perform. If you're a woman, you should find a man with a feat.

8.2885.

A man really depends on his women as they inspire him into war. A warrior should avoid women who don't inspire into death.

8.2898.

Prince examined Cinderella from feet to head, at first he saw legs, then her hips, then her breast... but he didn't manage to see the face, that's why he was foolish enough to run with that glass slipper. That lover of female legs didn't even manage to talk to her or ask her name.

8.3035.

A person sophisticated in life is persistent with women, patient with the elderly and honest with partners.

8.3203.

A feat is a big pleasure. A hero is joyful. A man without a feat is a sad sufferer.

8.3380.

The task of a man is to provide his woman with everything she needs. The task of a woman is to inspire her man into doing it.

8.3774. A successful man.

A woman's desires make a man better... A man has to work and think more and it makes him more noble. Besides, resisting the never ending female desires, he trains his Will and as is known, Will is the base of any success.

8.3803. Bluebeard.

Perhaps, the fairy tale about Bluebeard is the most cautionary tale for all women. A man is always a monster and it's necessary either to put up with it or simply not to know about it.

8.3804.

If a person doesn't seem like a monster to you, you just don't know him well. This person doesn't trust you and he never took off his mask in front of you.

8.3973.

A woman should understand that a normal male being is an adrenaline animal who sometimes get unbridled outbursts of rage during which a man should be left alone and it's necessary to ignore everything he may do or say...

If a man is deprived of adrenaline, he will soon turn into a eunuch incapable of reproduction and struggling.

8.4026.

The essence of intellectual symbiosis between a man and a woman is that men are better at seeing the whole, while women notice more details.

8.4113.

A man is significantly different from a woman, but often not for the better.

8.4216. Invaluable.

The more a man is ready to pay for a woman, the more he likes her... And he's ready to give anything for his beloved woman.

8.4327.

Men differ from each other only by their women.

8.4349.

It is quite easy to make a man fall in love with you: just do not stop him from lying and bragging and, preferably, encourage him enthusiastically from time to time…

8.4363. Flattery is water.

Men emaciate without flatter and women wither without it.

8.4392. The secret of love.

Men like to lie and be boastful, and they like women who are ready to really believe everything they say.

8.4448.

An artist cannot do without a muse... An artist without a muse won't be able to create and will die of hunger.

8.4455. About feminism again.

I'm ready to give my place of work to a woman, but in return she should give hers to me... otherwise, what am I supposed to do? And by the way, in wild nature the fair sex is often represented by men.

8.4459.

As a man, I support feminism and approve of equality. In every-thing... especially in expenses... And I'm terribly angry as not a single woman has ever given me flowers or asked me out to some restaurant... And by the way, I really want to be courted, kept, given presents and made love with for all those things...

8.4473.

Let's be honest. Have you ever met a decent man who wouldn't be a self-affected egoistic psycho that dreamed of conquering the world?

8.4498.

The only type of men who like chasing feminists are twerps, that's why feminists think that all men are twerps... Normal men are scared of feminist aggression... and chauvinists prefer to troll them.

8.4504. The last Hero and his Muse.

In the war between the two sexes the winner will be the one who won't give up. But if no one gives up, mankind will die out. And it occurred to me...they actually look for happiness. But alas, as long as the war goes on, no one can be happy. Besides, if women win, the heroic type of men will die out as Heroes never give up. Together with heroes Muses will die out as well as hunters, creators, warriors and finally...there will remain only very strange people resembling animals...

8.4513. Taming of an animal.

There's only one thing that a woman should know about a man: a man is ready to forgive a woman anything on the condition that she satisfies his sexual appetite and lets him lie and be boastful...

8.4514.

A man can be either carnivorous or graminivorous. A woman can rule an animal by sex, passion, tenderness and flattery. But ruling the graminivorous doesn't imply any particular skills.

8.4518.

There are two types of men: herbivores and carnivores. The herbivores are those who are goats and rams.

8.4541.

A conservative is the one who believes that a man should work, and a woman should be beautiful. Liberals are more sympathetic to sex minorities and insist that a woman should work .

8.4542. The illusion of beauty.

Love is an illusion. Love is the quickest and easiest way for a woman to become beautiful. A man in love is blind and feels her only by touch.

The illusory representation of the person you love is beautiful and perfect regardless of any external circumstances.

8.4605.

A man needs a woman, without a woman a man feels sad.

8.4628.

It's anyone else but herself that a woman blames for her problems. Weak men behave the same way.

8.4630. The best thing about a man is a woman.

8.4652. The base of love passion.

Men like to be boastful in women's presence, because in any healthy relationship a woman should admire her man, her admiration is the base of love and passion. If a man didn't manage to impress some woman, he'd better finish this relationship as it's hopeless.

8.4685.

A man doesn't feel like being with a woman who doesn't admire, respect or believe him. However, the same goes for women.

8.4785.

A man is a simpler version of a woman that was created to work for a woman and her descendants.

8.4788.

Men and women are meant for reproduction, and thus, for sex.

8.4825.

Men can be either aggressive or passive, passive men are not meant for sex and reproduction.

8.4827.

A man will be gentle with the woman who is loyal, pleasing and loving with him. Sex, love, gentleness and loyalty are the main female weapons that turn a man into a slave.

8.4988.

Many men marry only out of jealousy. A man can't stand the thought that his woman is not around him.

8.5092.

Once a man refuses to have sex, he can save a great deal of energy, time and money. These resources are enough to conquer the world. Thus, the choice is whether it's women or the world!

8.5193. A graphite control rod of a nuclear reactor.

The task of a woman is to be a catalyzer, to inspire a man into actions, into conquering the world, into work and personal growth. Besides, she wants him not to burst out, not to make irrevocable mistakes and not to commit suicide out of depression. The task of a muse is to keep a creator's working efficiency, helping him to create and cooling him off when he is so overwrought that is ready to burst or go crazy.

8.5194. A muse is an engineer.

A muse is an engineer whose task is to let off steam, put wood into firebox, watch the road and control the engine so that it would go the right way and not try to explode or go get into the wrong place.

8.5217.

What does a scared man do? He attacks, of course.

8.5230. A real male creature.

A wild man is indifferent to female demagogy, it's necessary to grab him by the testicles at once.

8.5611.

A man is a creator who is ready to create for those who love and admire him. A woman is the creature who is ready to love the one who impresses her and creates for her.

8.5763.

In a man's life, a woman performs the role of a graphite control rod of a nuclear reactor, she's a moderator and stabilizer.

8.5836. Doomed to loneliness.

A man of art cannot be prescribed any women as art demands love and any woman dislikes it when there's someone else to love besides herself.

The same can be said about philosophers and those who are passionate about what they do- all of them are doomed to loneliness...

8.5885.

Every man's heel of Achilles is some woman.

8.5906.

A woman can easily break a man, but decent men should not get broken because of women.

8.5943.

A woman feels bad without a man, and a man feels unbearably bad without a woman.

8.5944.

A man is an object of female admiration. If a man is not admirable, he's nothing for a woman.

8.5977. A man attacks so that a woman would run away.

8.5986.

A man is always doomed to be under female control, it can be either his Muse, or his Mother.

8.5987.

I've noticed that women on dating sites are in search of a really kind and good man... It's a naive and contradictory desire... It should be noticed that a good man is a carnivore... and it's love for his woman that makes him kind.

8.6144.

A man can get used to being ridden. If no one rides him, he will start to have a mope.

8.6145.

A poor person in love is wide-eyed, feeling as if something pressed him like a cigarette in the mouth...
...and it chews...and chews...

8.6536.

Thinking is very good for the brain, it becomes fir and beautiful. Beautiful brain is like abs, women like it very much (and men too).

8.6823. They like to give joy.

They lie because you like it...

8.6824.

They lie as they like it very much and it seems like sex to them.

8.6861.

The way to a man's heart is through love and gentleness, and the way to obesity is through stomach.

8.7106.

A person in love is one who is capable of doing foolish things.

8.7116.

The development of human civilization is caused by men's battle for women, food and EGO.

8.7129.

There's nothing more useful for a woman than a man who is guilty towards her.

8.7325.

Jealousy is a fear, fear of losing something priceless. But men often attack what they fear, so jealousy is often aggressive and even full of hatred.

8.7367. An insane man.

A woman needs a man who loves her, as she can rule such man and he can take care of her really skillfully. The signs of a man's love are the following: he regularly calls his woman and tries to meet, likes to touch her and hold hands, he cannot stand being without his woman or without hearing her voice for a while. He spends most of his money on her, besides it's not about any particular sum but what part of his income it is. He gives her lots of presents and attention. And if a relationship is new and there is novelty in it, these symptoms are many times more intense. If there are no symptoms of this kind, then it's not love but a simple desire to have sex without any unnecessary expenses.

Love drives crazy, if a person remains sane but plays into love, such person is a hypocritical creature. A few more signs of love include: kindness, respect, admiration for the partner, but these symptoms are easy to fake, unlike insanity.

8.7371.

A woman should either drive a man crazy or leave him as someone genetically incompatible with her.

8.7373.

The older one is, the harder it is for him to fall in love. With age, people become more freedom-loving and do not want to be slaves any longer, especially men.

8.7475.

A man needs a dream and a woman needs a man with a dream.

8.7508. The truth about men.

The older they are, the more cynical and chauvinistic they get, but also they become more hypocritical and wear masks...

8.7513.

Women hate chauvinists but all men are chauvinistic, that's why successful men are very hypocritical and have many different masks to choose from for every particular person they ever deal with.

8.7514. Female method.

If a man deliberately maintains distance from a woman he dates, it means he tries to manipulate her and evoke her passion to get control over her.

8.7525.

A man either loves a woman or takes her for a fool of a woman.

8.7559.

A genius differs from a psycho only by useful nature and constructive activity. Thus, any genius is a psycho but not every psycho is a genius. In order to turn a psycho into a genius it takes a good goal and deed. Psychos are fanatical and when they have some deed to serve, they will be the best loyal servants...
   Any man who is not deprived of vanity, irascibility, megalo-

mania etc, is a psycho...

8.7560.

It's very difficult to be a fanatic of some deed without being a psycho.

8.7562.

Any decent man (aka genius, sunlight, hero or simply alfa male) is a psycho doomed to self-destruction. But a woman-muse who is able to save him and turn him into sunlight- nuclear reactor as she will perform the role of graphite rods in the nuclear reactor and will help to escape an explosion and make the system work usefully.

8.7563.

On the one hand, women dislike psychos, but on the other hand, they simply can't use them properly... In essence, a psycho is the most useful type of man... a man "nuclear reactor", a man "sunlight" and a source of energy. The essence of a woman's art is about ruling a man to escape an explosion and self-destruction of the energetic pattern. It can be supposed that in the system where a man is a nuclear reactor, a woman is fuel- uranium and at the same time a ruling graphite rod.

8.7708.

Capitalism turns 70% of men into non-achievers, which negatively impacts demography and the institution of the family, females don't want to live with non-achievers.

8.7800. A monk.

An ocean of energy will be available for a man if he manages to stay away from women.

8.7805.

Everyone has the right to be oneself. The right to take off the mask and be a monster for a while.

8.8035. A homeless fledgling sparrow.

He fell for her because she gave him one while others refused. But then another one gave him one and he suddenly fell for her and forgot about the first one.

8.8036. A hungry chaffinch.

Nobody ever loved him, but this woman gave him one. Of course, soon he fell for her.

8.8037. A housing problem.

They often fall in love, because they have nowhere to live.

8.8039. Lookers-on see more than players.

A usual female delusion "I'm not like this, I'm another type" is also typical of men. It's better to eradicate this in yourself and don't resist attempts to become a cultured person.

8.8154. A monk of Shaolin.

As for sources of energy for a man... There are two variants: on the one hand, it's possible to find a normal female muse who is able to multiply energy, but this variant is not stable. The best variant is to get rid of women at all as if they are energy-sucking vampires... It would help to save personal energy.

8.8158.

A woman appreciates a man for the feelings she gets when he is near.

8.8173.

When male moose have rutting time they think only about females, while they are very sensible animals at any other season.

8.8335.

Intellectual and financial equality between men and women can kill love... Now, when a woman got no reasons to admire her man, how can she love him?

Why does she need to start a family with someone she doesn't consider the best one?

8.8393.

A man can have as many women as he is able to afford, and not a penny more.

8.8462.

Many men are chauvinistic enough to consider women sillier than they are. The essence of it is that no woman would be close with a man sillier than herself. A woman needs to love and admire her man... Thus, if a woman is smarter and better than you, she will never deal with you and that's why you've never known such women well enough.

8.8492. The story of Adam

When everything in your life is well, you don't need to evolve, that's why with enough luck a monkey would stay on a palm to carelessly eat bananas, but there wasn't enough luck. And one day this monkey fell from the palm and broke a paw so that it became impossible to climb up again to get bananas. There was nothing to eat but there were many carnivores around... This situation made the monkey "switch on the brain" and start to evolve. A bit later Adam met God, and if I'm not mistaken her name was Eve, but it's just rumor.

8.8493.

It's difficult to to evolve without any help, it takes a stick.

8.8511. Emancipation of a man.

Freedom from the practice of plural marriage was the act of setting men free from the necessity to marry every woman they sleep with. The more wives a man had, the more energy they consumed and deprived a man of any freedom.

8.8527.

The God who is not loved by anyone, turns into devil.

8.8569.

Love engenders kindness and we are kind to those who love us.

8.8570.

A woman should love her man as he is, with all his flaws and vices. Love will inspire the man, he will grow soft and the woman will be able create whoever she wants from him, for example, a Hero or a Hunter.

8.8571.

Any woman dreams of her man being kind to her. Kindness derives from love. If a woman loves her man, he's kind to her by default.

8.8687. An alpha male.

Everyone wants and loves something that doesn't have. That's why men who resemble women, have few chances for reproduction. In the soul of a real man there are even mechanisms that make him cultivate behavior that differs from female. Men often look at women and do things the opposite way.

8.8708. The practice of polygamy.

Polygamy is not profitable for most men and the government. In case of mass practice of polygamy there won't be enough women for men and it will lead to great social indignation. A woman is a tool for ruling and controlling a man, if there are not enough women so that some men are left without women, these men will soon become totally unruly and socially dangerous.

8.8750.

Desires of men differ from those of women, men like little taut pillows while women prefer soft big ones. It's easy to fall asleep on a soft big pillow by sinking in it with thoughts. While it's possible to stay away from sleep on a little pillow while thinking about the eternal.

8.8811.

Some boys are just like girls who try to find the sources of their problems in others. It's a delusion, all your problems live inside yourself.

9.1409.

It's very difficult for men to perform monotonous work that demands attentiveness.

9.2279.

A man who chases a woman resembles a hare who chases a fox.

9.2466.

Thinking style of men and women differs. Men prefer to think in solitude, while women do it in a team. Men are mostly interested in their own opinion, while women consider public opinion to be important. It happens because originally men were hunters and fishermen who had a lot of time to think in solitude, waiting for their prey, while women stayed in a big group of people doing the household chores and they had to think in a united collective mind without any opportunity to stay alone.

9.2752.

People are like children: they are not allowed to do what they love most. Doing what he is not allowed makes a man feel like a hero who has overcome his fear.

9.3770.

It is undesirable for a man to complain, a man should better forget about all his problems at once.

9.4353.

A worthy man doesn't have to think about women or waste time and efforts on them, he only should aim at perfection and women, fame and money will find the perfect one on their own.

9.4604.

The closer a man to perfection, the more he is loved by women and money.

9.4640.

Artists resemble women and works of art resemble children.

9.4725. The first admonition to an adult son.

It's education and business that should come first and only then apartments, women and dreams. The sources of income are more important than the sources of expenses.

9.4755.

A man cannot live alone. To be happy, he needs an Occupation to be proud of.

9.4894.

A man will fall for the woman who will give him a feat. Catching a beauty's heart is a great feat for a man.

9.4899.

Male bragging is part of the ritual dance, when the peacock, fluffing his tail, trying to delight the lady. The problem of "smart" women is that they do not admire ritual dances, they do not want to look admiringly at the male. This state of Affairs is very bad for sex and relationships in General.

9.4948. A hero in love.

With the help of sex a woman can give a man the thing that he needs most of all. - To feel himself a hero. A hero is joyful.

The source of joy is joyful. Nowadays, men don't get enough reasons to be heroes, there's no one to bring joy to and no one to make happy. We love those whom we make happy. It flatters self-affection and vanity. In essence, it's a natural drug by using which a woman can make a man fall for her and control him.

9.4953. Perhaps, as well as female ones.

The most villain-like male character is killjoy and hypocrite.

9.4983.

A man really needs to be admired, without female admiration he fades away.

9.4988.

Generally, both witches and muses make positive impact on men. Muses inspire them with love, witches do it with freedom.

9.5033.

A man's manner to be boastful is analogous to a peacock's feathers. A peacock displays feathers as part of a courtship ritual to attract a peahen. That's why, biologically it's silly to criticize a man for being boastful and lying. How else can he manage reproduction?

9.5070.

It's very dangerous for a man to be weak and silly. If such man gets into a woman's hands, he will be doomed to suffer.

9.5239.

Persistence is what makes a man a man. Verity is something that never gives up.

9.5240.

Men tend to listen to reason, that's why women consider them to be unfeeling... It's only because the function of men is to overcome fears. And feelings mostly mean fears, that's why real men are always quite unfeeling.

9.5252.

Men are vain. Creators are always vain. It's impossible to create without being vain. Creators love only their own deeds and those who love their deeds. Thus, if a woman needs not only sex from a man, but if she wants him to love her and create for her, she will have to love him and his dream.

9.5259. Sense and sentiments.

"Don't want" is typical women. Men prefer to think categorically "need to" or "don't need to"

9.5261.

A hero is someone who kills fears. Women are scared of fears and are fond of heroes.

9.5266.

Life, just like women, loves persistent people.

9.5268.

Men don't love women who don't love them, this is the reason for most divorce suits.

9.5269.

As a rule, men love in return, they are unable to love first.

9.5270.

The only motive for a man to tolerate a woman and waste time and resources on her is that she loves him. While he loves her in return.

9.5284.

I know three types of men. The first one is creators, those who are loved. The second one are demons, those who are not loved. And the third type of men is "nothing with a bow from one side".

9.5297.

Strong male effect. He only needs to look at her and she's already pregnant, even if only in her dreams.

9.5298.

A strong male is very useful in many ways for female health. A stout-hearted man, just like some holy spirit who can make a woman feel heavenly and even experience immaculate conception... This vision can make a woman excited. Her immune system galvanizes the body into living, health and youth. The reason is simple- a healthy female is more sexually attractive, it would be undesirable to miss a good variant for reproduction.

10.1863. 12 lines of life.

There are 12 ways of suffering and only one way of joy.

10.6698.

Too much sex makes a man lazy and cowardly. In the end, he gets used to pleasure and loses interest in women, and in everything else in the world.

10.7211. I'm perfect.

A boy can't communicate with normal women, but he can with prostitutes. The reason is cowardice, pride, and a desire for control. Losing control causes him to panic and demoralize.

10.7213. A closed cul-de-SAC?

A boy whose father was a dependent person and whose mother

was a dominant one will grow up admiring strong women on the one hand and hating them on the other, trying at all costs not to become a dependent person. Weak women such a boy will despise.

10.7864.

A man in a struggle with his woman grows up... a woman turns a boy into a man.

10.7882.

A man who is focused on his fear does not feel or pay attention to his woman.

10.7883. Love is courage.

If a man loves, the fear inside him disappears, and the woman, seeing his love, automatically falls in love with him. Women know that love is when there is no fear.

10.7909.

When a man goes headlong into his problems, a woman goes mad with pain from loneliness and puts him before a choice: problems or her. A man in love should say that all problems are nonsense, and turn his attention to the woman.

10.7960.

It is desirable for a man to match the dreams of his woman in order to deserve her admiration. Female admiration is very invigorating and motivating.

10.8006.

Empathy is a woman's feeling, because it makes a person run away from himself, makes him dependent on a stronger one. It is empathy that makes women dependent on men. A strong and courageous man is selfish and withdrawn.

10.8010. A person who is happy to be around.

When a man is narcissistic, self-confident, fearless, cold, fiercely masculine... all people who have empathy, and in particular women, fall into euphoric joy next to such a person.

10.8011.

A manly man will not even raise an eyebrow when he sees a beautiful woman, but he will be kind and affectionate, for there is no fear in him. Such restraint, like a magnet, will attract a woman to him.

10.8013.

A woman feels fear empathically and is sensitive to fear. And a man is insensitive and courageous, this protects him from fear. In order for a woman not to go mad with fear, she needs an insensitive, self-confident man, and a man needs to trust his woman to get information about threats and trends in the outside world. At the same time, a man should clearly understand that in General this information is exaggerated by an order of magnitude and it is not necessary to indulge all the fears and desires of his woman.

10.8145.

A man needs to think because he doesn't feel anything. And a woman does not need to think, she has an intuition that thinking only hinders, generating unnecessary fears.

10.8175.

It is better for a man to love himself or his ideas and goals. Concentrating your love on a woman is very dangerous. We turn into what we love. Women are full of fears. Falling in love with a woman beyond measure, a man risks drowning in fear. A woman who falls in love risks losing her fear.

10.8224.

Doubt is a woman's property. The firmness of the decision is a man's property. Doubt breeds fear.

10.8597.

When a woman treats a strong man with compassion, admiration, care, and tenderness... he melts.

10.8943. Curve.

An idealist is a person who really wants to achieve perfect symmetry in the family, turning his half into himself. But the second half of it turns out to be some pathetic parody of the first half, as a result, the entire structure is distorted.

10.9177.

Men are afraid of beautiful women because of greed... Hair stands on end, as you can imagine how much such a pleasure can cost.

10.9288.

A man dreams of a woman who would support him in all his feelings, even in mistakes, depressions, failures and despair. A woman, in turn, dreams of a man who does not need to be supported, because the man is healthy and heavy, and the woman is weak and fragile.

10.9462.

Jean and the mermaid are very similar metaphorical images that live in the dream of their illusions. Reality causes them pain that only love can save them from. If Gina or the mermaid Wake up and not give them love, they will go wild with fear and pain.

10.9464.

A man is the Creator of beauty, the Creator of flowers, and a woman is a butterfly that flits around flowers, rejoicing and giving joy. The joy that a butterfly gives to flowers inspires flowers to grow.

10.9534.

It should be realized that a touchy man is a small child who loves himself, and he uses a woman as a source of his pleasure. And if this pleasure does not happen, he resents it.

10.9872.

It seems to the proud man that he owes something to those whom he loves, respectively, they owe him. People think he gives because he loves, and he's a liar ... just a greedy moneylender who lends love at huge interest rates.

8.1904.3.

A man is a person who is meant to do something.
A man is a person who is busy with doing something.
He who is busy with some deed, is beautiful.

8.2390.1.

The more a man resembles a woman, the less he is suitable for reproduction.

10.10202. Unity of Yin and Yang.

Women are dominated by the need to complete the Gestalt, that is, to form patterns and complete forms. In men, the desire for knowledge and expansion dominates. By connecting, a woman and a man achieve harmony... a man captures new territories, and a woman motivates the construction of new walls and borders. Women are formulaic and limited in thinking. Men, on the contrary, do not recognize patterns and restrictions.

10.10286. A low-flying bird.

The male peacock is beautiful, but flies poorly. I spent all my energy on feathers, poor boy.

10.10564.

Woman is the soft that surrounds the hard, dominating it. A man is a solid that fills the soft.

10.12337.

A woman needs a man who has a beautiful dream and is not afraid to pursue it.

10.12776.

A woman, of course, likes to awaken a child in a man, but it would be better if she awakened a man in a child. Children are capricious and irresponsible. Children are angry and aggressive.

10.13020.

A woman can save a boy from pride and voluptuousness by limiting his pleasure and access to sex. In the absence of a woman, a man will deteriorate from an overabundance of Masturbation.

10.13367.

A man is a proud fire, and a woman is a vestal priestess whose job it is to ensure that the eternal fire never dies down. The vestal should know that fire is dangerous and should not be overfed.

10.13402.

Men, of course, are proud demons, creatures of the very depths of hell, but don't think that women are much better. Woman is the moon, the cause of the volcanic activity of the planet Earth. The Moon is responsible for the atmosphere and climate on our planet.

10.13896.

In a relationship with a woman, a male Builder should not strive to build a house once or make repairs, but constantly build, destroy, and repair. You can't stop. If there is nothing to build or repair, the old one will have to be destroyed.

10.13906. Deceptive desire.

The desire to make an idol out of a woman is the desire of a Genie to become a slave to his jug. And the gin itself obsessively sticks to the jug, wanting to become its slave under the guise of possessing it.

10.13951.

Theoretically, the real pride of a man and the illusory pride of a woman are quite compatible.

10.13978.

As soon as a woman feels power, she also feels lust. Only when a man senses lust does he feel power.

10.13987.

The fact that a man drank (alcohol) speak of his fear of pain, that is, cowardice, deceitfulness and weakness of spirit.

10.13988.

You see, if you are a Queen, it is not for you to fight for men, but for them to fight for you. Of course, you can also choose your hero, but then you need to know what their heroes are. The hero is honest, courageous, great in his goals, not a slave to Vice. The slave of Vice is not a hero, but a coward and a weak man. By the way, lust and idolatry are also a Vice.

10.14022.

A woman, inflamed with passion for a pathetic man, thinks that she will be able to give him strength. But this is a lie. In fact, sensing weakness, a woman craves power, wants to take a dominant position, automatically puts a man in a passive position, further aggravating the slavery of his vices and powerlessness.

10.14074.

A man in love, filling the life of his woman with joy, turns both himself and her into a drug addict. The same thing happens with children. The reason is that a man himself can not control his thirst for pleasure and uses his loved ones as their sources of pleasure. From the fear of losing a dose of the drug, a person falls into anger, fear, and procrastination. Out of fear, this person tries to over-control and take care of loved ones.

10.14249.

A real man must have an idea that he serves. If a man doesn't have an idea, it means that he is defective. If a man wants to turn his woman into an idea, this is also bad, because it will condemn the idol to suffering and turn it into a slave.

10.14280.

A man, falling into depression, tries to turn his woman into his only source of pleasure. From the outside, it's like a vampire try-ing to drink all the blood of its victim.

10.14305.

A coward is very hungry for love. For fear that he will not have enough love, he is ready to promise anything. Fear is greed, the thirst for insufficiency.

10.14336. Man test.

All the female traits that usually infuriate men are just intuitive ways to experience a man. A woman checks whether this man has patience, courage, wisdom, and love.

10.14353. Black hole.

The average man is a void that greedily sucks in love. It is worth feeling sorry for such a person, giving him a piece of love, as he will instantly suck you whole, like a vampire drinking all your energy and time.

10.14474. Scenario 666.

A man turns his wife into his idol and source of energy. Love (lust) gives him strength and saves him from fear. At first everything goes fine, but then it all generates greed, addiction, exhaustion, over-control, intolerance ... sublimating to work and personal life. Because of his idealism, a person inevitably falls into pride and begins to experience problems at work and with health, panics and even more begins to seek help from the "mother", who has already exhausted emotionally by this time. Without getting energy, a man falls into despair and depression, is terribly offended and begins to hate his wife and the world in General. Depression is accompanied by procrastination, loss of strength, and hopelessness. The business is rolling downhill, the family is falling apart... loneliness, disease, decay, and death.

"Is there a way out?"

- Need a backup power generator and a miracle pill for pride (lust for power, overcontrol, greed, idealism). This person's beliefs are incompatible with life.

10.14485. Circle of pleasures.

A man who has made an idol of his wife becomes dependent on sex, it seems to him that sex gives him strength and energy. In fact, it's all self-deception. In reality, this person is afraid of losing his wife, and since he himself views her as a source of pleasure, he subconsciously thinks that she also views him in the same way. It seems to him that if she does not have a crazy orgasm or she is not happy 24 hours a day, then she is unhappy and will definitely run away from him. The idea that My darling CAN run away is maddening.

"Is he a fool?"

– Rather, ignorant, he just did not say as a child that less is better than more. And now he doesn't trust anyone.

10.14487.

Men's lust is not even a thirst for pleasure, but a thirst for power. It seems to him that the more pleasure he brings to a woman, the more she will love him. Alas, this is a lie. From an overabundance of pleasure, a woman will quickly get used to and lose interest in a man.

10.14488.

A man is fixated on female pleasure not for the sake of a woman, but for the sake of his own self-esteem and sense of power. Having given pleasure, he imagines that now this woman is his, and will not run away anywhere else. The feeling of power intoxicates and gives delight to the soul.

10.14525.

A man always lies to a woman that she can't do without him. Spoils, teaches to comfort, tries to bind to itself pleasure, money, pain... YOU will not be able to live without me, it will be bad for you... the man lies. Smart women laugh at this lie, stupid women are afraid and cry. However, women are no less liars than men.

10.14537.

Men especially like to fight their fears with the help of women.

But that's stupid, isn't it?
– Indeed, many men can't be called anything but cowards and fools.

10.14538.

A man tries to own a woman through the pleasure he gives her. The more he gave her pleasure, the more he owned her. The man himself enjoys the sublimation of a sense of power. The more power a man feels, the greater his pride and strength becomes. A woman, intuitively adjusting the level of her joy, can control the demon of pride.

10.14844.

Abomination is pride. If a person tells you about love with a sad expression on his face – it is not love, because love is admiration and joy.

10.14847.

A woman is necessary for a man who has no brains of his own. When a man doesn't have ideas that are worthy of love, a woman comes on the scene and finds something useful for him. In the absence of a woman, a man can easily morally decompose and become a slave to vices.

10.14887.

When a proud man becomes attached to his love, both suffer in chains. When love breaks its chains and finds freedom, it rejoices. The proud man, howling in pain, runs after her, catches her back and puts her on a chain.

10.14961. Scenario # 13.

The tyrant husband (order, firmness) in the thirst for power over his wife (chaos, water), creates an unbearable environment at home. Wanting power, the husband forbids his wife to work and in every way restricts her freedom. Unable to endure constant negativity, the wife finds solace in various addictions (alcohol, drugs, TV shows, the Internet) and loses the ability to learn. In parallel, the father takes out his aggression on the children, but compensating them with gifts, turns them into pleasure-dependent addicts, reducing their sensitivity threshold. Having ceased to enjoy ordinary things, children also begin to look for pleasure in vices. As a result, the father of the family (a light and white angel) tears his hair on his head, accusing his wife that the children went to her, and in General, he is one normal person here.

10.14966. You need to take care of yourself.

A man tries to dominate hard, belittling women's self-esteem. A woman should respond to such an attempt at power with righteous anger and send it to hell. If a woman doesn't say anything, anxiety will sublimate into guilt and fear. In General, all this is stressful and harmful to health. A man should behave similarly.

10.14985. The vessel of evil is the Keeper of fire.

A woman is a vessel of evil, but not evil itself. Evil is a man, and a woman, depending on her experience and perfection, can turn this evil into light. A man is an oil with a wick that can be poured into a vessel, set on fire and then it will turn into a candle that gives light. The meaning of a woman, as a vessel of fire, is to store and feed the fire, keeping it alive, while not allowing it to turn into an all-consuming fire.

10.14992.

A man keeps a woman around him with a whip or carrot, which makes her life hell. Food should be balanced and harmonious. A healthy diet is when there is a little bit of everything.

10.15033.

Usually, when a man says about a woman that she does not love him well, it means that he is a greedy, proud man who is always short of everything. However, women's greed does not differ much from men's.

10.15077.

The philosophy of Syntalism will be especially useful for women who suffer from the despotism and pride of men.

10.15394.

A man is someone who inspires confidence in a woman.

10.15413.

The proud man is somewhat like a sperm. He seeks to enter the world and, having impregnated it, begin to change it. Once in the world of a woman, he drags a woman with him, changing her entire universe.

10.16157.

I know two types of demons created by love. One yearns for love, and it turns out to be perfect. Such a ghoul sucks energy, trying to be good and doing something useful. Another vampire cannot be perfect, and he flies into a rage, and the power to extort love. You can recognize both ghouls by their hunger and the cold emptiness in their eyes.

10.16158.

A vampire is dependent on love and turns violent when he feels that he is not loved. However, if you love a vampire from afar, it will be quite useful for society essence.

10.16263.

Everything that deprives a man of courage makes him a slave to fear, vices, and people.

10.16530.

Many men unconsciously provoke a conflict between their wives and their mother-in-law in order to get rid of their mother's power by their wife's hands. At the same time, the man himself remains formally good, his conscience does not torment him, and his mother even feels sorry for him.

10.16732.

A selfish man who is over-loved by his mother will find a passive woman who will love him instead of his mother, and he will rule over her. A woman will periodically snarl and rebel, and a man will be offended that they do not love him enough and do not forgive his shortcomings.

10.16767. From the lives of madmen.

The proud tyrant, dominating and mocking his relatives, is offended that he is ill-loved, accuses his slaves of ingratitude, and for attempts at rebellion declares them scoundrels and madmen.

10.17329.

A woman always reflects her man honestly. A man who is dissatisfied with his woman is a liar and a proud man, unable to accept himself as he is. In fact, it is an inferiority complex, compensated by narcissism.

10.17333.

If a woman does not like how her man behaves, you need to put the question like this: either divorce, or go to a family psychologist.

10.17719.

Why does a man lie? So that the woman doesn't swear. As a result, the woman swears even more. Women can't stand lying and cowardly men.

10.17740.

In relationships, the greater negative effect comes from men, women prefer to adjust.

10.18287. Mars and Venus.

There are two types of men: the former are similar to the planet Earth, and the latter are similar to The sun. There are also two types of women: the first look like the moon, and the second like the Earth. When a man is the sun, a woman is the earth, and there is love and fruitfulness in her. When a man is the earth, a woman is the moon, and there is less joy in her life. On the other hand, there are a great many planets and satellites, the example of the Earth and the moon is a good example of love, there are many other examples with a sadder outcome.

10.18417.

Man should not be the sun. The sun is pride that eclipses the stars. A man should be a fruitful earth, and a woman should be a moon full of beauty and mystery. The sun is a man's dream.

10.18450.

When a man truly loves a woman, it kills the fear in him. In the absence of fear, a man acquires the ability to grow and expand. In the absence of fear, a man becomes courageous and joyful. A woman's empathy allows her to feel what a man feels, and this fills her soul with delight.

10.18816.

A man The proud man sees submission to his lust for power as a manifestation of love. True, this love is false, and rather like fear. Such a man will experience insufficiency and permanent hunger for love.

10.18992.

Saturn is a symbol of distance from love, bound by chains of vices.

10.19007.

You can't dominate both at work and at home. You can't control someone you love at all. You need to choose whether you are the master of the house or the outside world.

10.19234.

From cowardice, men can not normally part with a woman, saying "I do not want to", but always tell that they are either unworthy, or they do not like and do not understand.

10.19235.

Men's talk about their own unworthiness does not frighten women, because they like to rule and feel like heroines.

10.19240.

Drug addiction (thirst pleasure) it can make a proud man abandon his home, possessions, and wife, which have already become part of his Ego. But a little later, when the addiction occurs, the man will be overcome by fear in the form of guilt and inability to return.

10.19241.

A proud man cannot directly abandon a woman, because for him it is an act of metaphorical suicide, the loss of a part of his Ego. So to leave a woman, a man tells three types of stories: he is not worthy of her, she does not love him, she is not worthy of him.

10.19242. Suicide.

The proud man makes all his pleasure a part of his one Ego. A woman creates a sub-personality for every pleasure, and when love dies, she kills this sub-personality.

10.19384.

It is difficult for a proud man to swear with his wife, because he really does not want to scold himself.

10.19410. Three women's ideas.

He doesn't understand me. He must. It will change. However, not only women's.

10.19416.

Men do not know how to apologize, because they believe that women should apologize first. A man's apologies are rude and unpleasant.

10.19501.

The burning Bush is a symbol Jesus, the symbol of a man in love with a higher power An idea, and not afraid of the love of women and other people. Women's love is a flame that can easily destroy a man who has no higher love.

10.19511.

A woman tries to control a man with her passion. A man who is dependent on women's love is doomed to communicate with women who will try to actively dominate him.

10.19523.

The male Creator is imperfect, he still needs to grow and train. Woman perfect from the very beginning and ready to create a person.

10.19581.

The family can be seen as a nuclear reactor, where the man is nuclear fuel, and women are the control rods. Women's task: to heat up the system, generating a chain reaction, while simultaneously holding it back from explosion and avalanche-like disintegration. This state of Affairs directs a woman to order, and a man to explosive expansion and fruitful growth. The woman's task is to make sure that the system performs useful work, and there are no energy leaks.

10.19610.

A man needs fire energy, absorbing the female love of his mistresses, he gains strength for expansion. However, in order to maintain and structure his income, he needs a wife, otherwise he will spend all his money on entertainment, vices and women.

10.20106.

A man who will not limit and be jealous of a woman is a strong, courageous and wise man. Cowards and ignoramuses are jealous and petty.

10.20115.

Men whose souls are filled with pride and narcissism are doomed to have big problems in the family, their wives will always be sick, and give them a lot of problems. As for children, there will be no special joy from children. However, proud and narcissistic women are not very happy either.

10.21012.

In the absence of self-respect and lack of external recognition, a weak man will seek solace in vices, alcoholism, drug addiction... his character will begin to show aggression, self-love, resentment of the whole world, contempt for others, distrust of people, nihilism and criticism of life. In fact, all these features of the worldview are characteristic of pride and ignorance. To combat pride, you need self-restraint, fasting, work, reading, learning, and humility.

10.22093.

The husband's intolerance of his wife's relatives or friends is related to the desire for power and the realization of the thesis "divide and rule".

10.22605.

A man with vices is very useful for a woman to self-justify her own vices and raise her self-esteem.

10.22631.

Proud women like cowardly men, they like to rule. On the other hand, pride is a source of great suffering.

10.22641.

Anyone who seeks help from women is a fool. Trying to hide behind a skirt or find comfort from a woman turns a man into a coward, depriving him of strength. You should rely on yourself. You should seek comfort in yourself. When hope is pushed out, it creates fear.

AFTERWORD

10.22334. A grain of sand.

Variothoughts is sand, not gold. According to Syntalism, our world is built of sand, not gold. The most valuable thing is sand, sand is bread, and gold is salt.

10.22742.

Variothoughts books should be read slowly, chewing every thought carefully. Truth is that which has extension properties, and falsehood is pride, that is, an avid rush.

10.22339.

There are no questions that cannot be answered in the Variothoughts. The Variothoughts is an endless source of inspiration for hearts searching for truth.

10.22266. Nutcracker.

Breaking stereotypes and patterns. Variothoughts is a brain-crushing book, the meaning of which is to achieve the integrity of the mind. First, all beliefs should be destroyed in the dust, and then it will all stick together and enlightenment will come.

10.22554. The living and the dead book.

In the original, Variothoughts is the ideal of the perfection of truth, but the ideal is dead and, therefore, there is no joy in it. To bring back the joy of life to Variothoughts, I decided to salt the bread. Salt-free bread is too sweet. In Variothoughts translations, I threw a couple of spoons of chaos. My act of monstrous vandalism led to the loss of 20% of the meaning, and made the texts very strange and obscure. You will call me a scoundrel and a vandal, but I don't think so ... On the contrary, I believe it made the texts charming, created artificial barriers ... Now, to understand the texts of Variothoughts and find the truth, you have to smash your head and think. Thinking is joyful.

10.15530.

The basis of speech is truth. Cognition of truth should begin with clarifying the meaning of words.

10.16833.

The main feature of Variothoughts is its unprecedented honesty. No censorship of thoughts, absolute freedom of ideas and words.

5.412.

Variothoughts is a book for those who save their time. Ready-made Lego cubes used to put together any ideas and goals. The DNA and RNA of thought.

3.2212. Attainment of truth.

A comprehensive attainment of reality occurs by knowledge's thinning of its tiniest degree of detail.

3.2213.

Unity is hidden in differences. You unite by disuniting. Holding one onto another, the infinitely small becomes the infinitely big.

10.6168.

The Variothoughts is a basic library of DNA of thought, loading it into the brain can solve any problem. Any dreams, any goals will be available to you, thanks to the philosophy of Syntalism.

3.1971.

Variothoughts implements divergent thought algorithms in order to come again to unity through a multitude. Many grows out of one and one grows again out of many.

3.2211.

Soundness is the ability to dynamically examine things from different perspectives.

3.2216.

Having reached its limit, knowledge transforms into will. What is the limit of knowledge? – Faith.

10.21243. Love of truth.

The meaning of human life is to overcome infinite loneliness and find infinite love.

ABOUT THE AUTHOR

8.2479.

SoloINC (anc.greek "combining the uncombinable", keeper of the grain")

Soloinc Logic, philosopher from the city of Sofia. Soloinc (Diamond Solo / Solodilov Dmitry), Bulgarian psychologist and Stoic philosopher. Supporter of the merger of logical and sensory methods of cognition. He considers the connection of traditional philosophies with modern science. He is the founder of the cyber-philosophy of Syntalism (Quantum Nanophilosphy), which considers the problems of philosophy, sociology, psychology and economics in terms of systemic cybernetics and logic.

Soloinc is not the first, but the last philosopher. Evangelist and cyberpunk guru. The author of more than 73 thousand original ideas and thoughts. Main books: "Variothoughts", "Diamond Stoic", "Theory of Existence", "Money Bible", "Quantum Philosophy", "Mathematics and Progression", "Velerechie", "The Device of the Mind", "Royal Buffoon", "Liberastia" , "Surrotic", "Surfutur" and others, in total more than 888 books.

3.1753.

In fact, Variothoughts is very tedious. I have sought the truth all my life, then I found it and concealed it in a different place. Variothoughts is an intellectual quest and a mosaic of truth, broken into thousands of pieces. I found the truth in plain sight and concealed it back as well as before… What's the point? It's a game or a way to kill boredom. We live eternally and boredom turns our life into hell. I want to save you from sufferings for some reason...

10.21128. Soloinc Music

Soloinc Music is a stunningly beautiful integrity of music and text, admiring metaphors and secret meanings. Soloinc Music is a pleasure for living minds who have dedicated their lives to the search for beauty and truth. Soloinc Music awakens the minds and ignites the heart. Everyone will find joy and strength to live in it.

10.2341. A realistic mysticism.

The genre of poetry and music of Soloinc is a mystical realism. Most Soloinc songs are mystical ballads or religious hymns, prophecies, and insights. Soloinc lyrics are always metaphors and mystical signs. They cannot be taken literally. These are grains of sand in which entire worlds are hidden. All words are the opposite. To understand the meaning of the Variothoughts texts you need to read from bottom to top, from right to left.

Syntalism - Generative Quantum Nanophilosphy

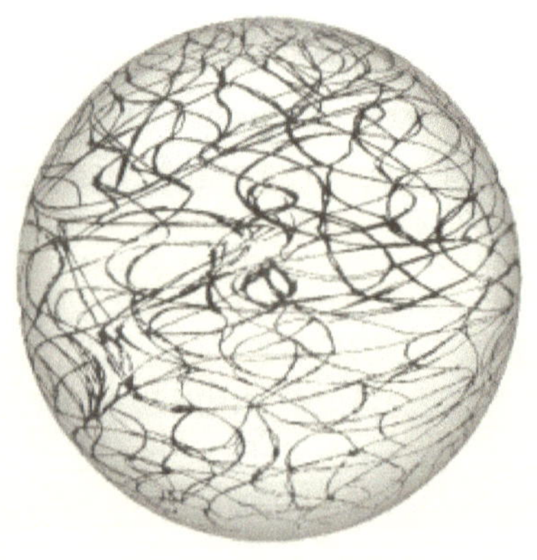

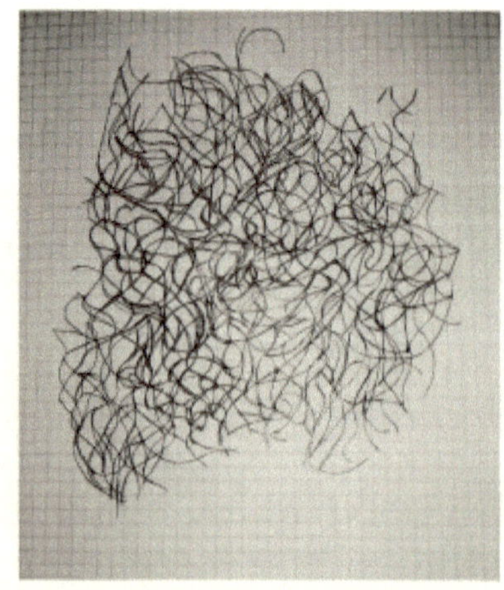

10.19296.

The philosophy of Syntalism was inspired by the poetry of life, expressed in the poems of such poets as Shakespeare, Robert Burns, Williams Blake, Pasternak, Lermontov, Mayakovsky, Velimir Khlebnikov, Paul Eluard, Andrey Bely, Alexander Blok, Voznesensky, Asadov, Gutseriev, Anna Akhmatova, Tsvetaeva, and others. Where if the philosopher had not come, the poet would have been there. Poets are like rays of light showing the way to thinkers.

5.782. Syntalism is the philosophy of the 5G generation.

Small thoughts are the philosophical system built in the millimeter wave range. Syntalism is 5G philosophy in the millimeter wave range built according to generative genetic algorithms.

5.767.

In Variothoughts, conceptualization follows the generative genetic algorithm.

10.22348.

Syntalism is a philosophy that connects the unconnected with the goal of achieving integrity. Integrity is truth. To know the truth, the mind must cultivate tolerance and humility.

5.783.

Variothoughts is structured as a phased antenna array that ensures a dynamic horizontal and vertical growth of thought according to the generative algorithm and makes it possible to create different-sized logic data arrays. This solution minimizes energy consumed to maintain the integral information field. Variothoughts is a system of small cells in the millimeter wave (super-small thought) range in which the size of cells and their interaction structure are dynamic in nature.

10.3109. Unified system of knowledge.

The philosophy of Syntalism is by far the most perfect and clear philosophy, revealing the nature of being. Syntalism is like an ocean containing all other philosophies and religions. Syntalism understands and explains any point of view, agrees with everyone and loves everyone, considers everyone beautiful. Thousands of points of view, uniting into streams and rivers, turn into an ocean of Synthism.

Variothoughts Collectible Books

4.3423. Sand vs truth?

A book's collectable from the Variothoughts series costs only 1 cubic meter of real estate property. It is a very delicious price for something priceless.

3153.

God loves collectors as they give work to many creators...

6.6033.

The electronic version of Variothoughts is huge but printed versions are more complete and this book's collectables and handmade versions are unique in their completeness. Each of the author's gift manuscripts of Variothoughts is handmade and customized, that's why it includes even the latest texts that exist only in rough copies and have not yet been published anywhere.

10.22513.

Friends, I have not sold any Variothoughts collectibles yet. Pride rules people, that is cowardice and greed. There are very few courageous and intelligent people. He who is brave and buys the first book is very lucky. The first collector's copy of Variothoughts is a great value. Each collection book is registered and numbered. However, there will never be many of them, if I sell such books at least a few pieces a year, it will be good.